All rights reserved.

From Empires to Exile: A Brief Uyghur History

• •• •• • •

"Those who cannot remember the past are condemned to repeat it."

— George Santayana

Those who succumbed to foreign influences abandoned their names and heritage, facing servitude and disgrace. Our noble sons and daughters became slaves, our traditions faded, and the proud Turkic spirit diminished. Let this be a warning: divided, we shall fall; united, we shall thrive

—Bilge Khagan

From Empires to Exile: A Brief Uyghur History

• •• • •• •• • •

   This book represents my personal understanding and interpretation of Uyghur history, drawn from extensive research and consultation of numerous historical texts. While I strive for accuracy and have provided citations wherever applicable, I do not claim to hold the authority of absolute truth regarding Uyghur history. History is a complex and multifaceted subject, open to varying interpretations, and this work reflects my perspective based on available information.
   This book is intended for readers who are beginners in learning about Uyghur history. It seeks to provide a clear and engaging introduction to the subject, offering foundational knowledge that can inspire further exploration and study.

   For simplicity and continuity, I use the term *Uyghurs* throughout this book to describe both modern Uyghurs and their ancestors. Readers should note, however, that the ancestors of the Uyghurs identified themselves by different names, such as *Turks*, *Uyghurs*, or other terms found in historical records, depending on the era and cultural context. This choice is made for narrative clarity and is not intended to impose anachronistic labels.

   In this book, the term *East Turkistan* is used to reflect the historical and cultural identity of the Uyghur homeland, which is officially referred to as the Xinjiang Uyghur Autonomous Region in modern China. This terminology honors the region's rich Turkic heritage and its significance to the Uyghur people.

   Many of the historical illustrations in this book have been AI-generated to offer visualizations of the lives, culture, and context of Uyghur ancestors and their history. These images are creative representations intended to enhance the reader's engagement and understanding, not precise historical reconstructions.

   I would like to express my deepest gratitude to all the historians, authors, and translators who have researched and shared Uyghur history, making it accessible to English-speaking audiences. Their work, cited and referred to throughout this book, has been invaluable in shaping my understanding and providing the foundation for this endeavor.

   This work is offered with humility and the hope that it contributes to a broader understanding of Uyghur history. Readers are encouraged to approach this subject with an open mind and consult additional sources to form their own perspectives.

From Empires to Exile: A Brief Uyghur History

• •• •• • •

The modern Uyghur people, enduring severe repression today, are the inheritors of a rich and multifaceted heritage. Their lineage traces back to ancient Turkic tribes and significant groups like the Tocharians, known for their urban planning and artistic traditions, and the Saka, who contributed to trade, military strategies, and metallurgy in Central Asia. This diverse ancestry has shaped the Uyghur identity over centuries, linking them to the region they have called home for millennia.

In the 8th century, the Uyghur Khaganate became the center of Turkic geopolitical power, governing vast territories from Mongolia to the Tarim Basin, synonymous with modern-day East Turkistan, and reaching into modern Kazakhstan. As key players along the Silk Road, they facilitated trade and cultural exchange, enriching the region's cosmopolitan character. After losing their capital to the Kyrgyz in 840, the Uyghur and other Toquz Oghuz tribes migrated to modern East Turkistan, together with their local brethren, establishing new centers of culture and power.

In the 10th century, Islam became central to Uyghur identity during their integration into the Karakhanid Empire, one of the earliest Islamic Turkic states. This period marked their transformation into a unique community within the Islamic world, forming alliances with powers like the Abbasid Caliphate and the Seljuk Sultanate. These themes of resilience and adaptability resonate throughout their history.

The Uyghurs contributed significantly to intellectual traditions. Figures like Mahmud al-Kashgari, author of the *Dīwān Lughat al-Turk*, and Yusuf Has Hajib, writer of *Kutadgu Bilig*, exemplify their cultural achievements. Their homeland reveals advanced civilizations with archaeological treasures, agricultural innovations, and thriving trade systems. They also pioneered printing technology in the 9th century, establishing early centers of printed text production.Despite current hardships, the Uyghurs' cultural and ancestral heritage remains a source of pride and resilience. This legacy inspires their ongoing struggle for survival, justice, and dignity. Their history stands as a testament to their achievements and a beacon for their aspirations.

The cover of this book features Mahmud al-Kashgari's 11th-century world map, taken from his monumental work *Dīwān Lughāt al-Turk*. This map offers a rare glimpse into the Turkic worldview of the era.

Introduction: The Uyghur People - Heritage, Struggle, and Legacy

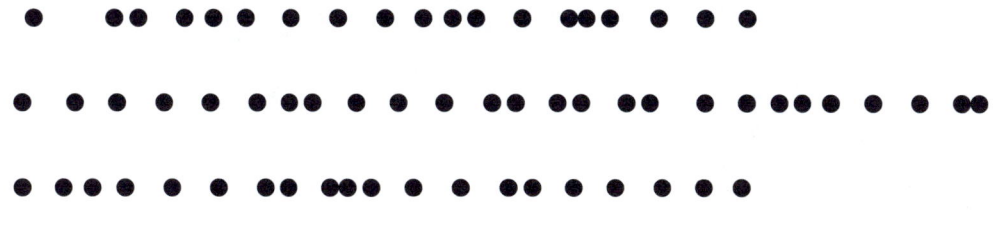

The Uyghurs are a Turkic people primarily located in East Turkistan, also known as the Xinjiang Uyghur Autonomous Region (XUAR) of China, as well as in Central Asian states such as Kazakhstan, Kyrgyzstan, and Uzbekistan. As a people with deep historical roots in Central Asia, the Uyghurs share linguistic, cultural, and ethnic ties with other Turkic groups.

The XUAR, officially designated by the Chinese constitution as an autonomous region for the Uyghur people, experiences limited autonomy in practice. Although Chinese government policies ostensibly grant ethnic minorities self-governance, the region remains tightly controlled by Beijing, particularly in governance, cultural expression, and religious practice. Over the past two decades, repression of the Uyghur population has intensified, especially under Xi Jinping's administration. Despite its designation as an autonomous region, Uyghur self-governance remains largely symbolic, with substantive authority retained by Beijing.[1,2]

The name Uyghur has a debated etymology, with early interpretations provided by Mahmud al-Kashgari, an 11th-century Uyghur scholar and author of *Dīwān Lughāt al-Turk*, a dictionary of Turkic languages and cultures. While Kashgari did not explicitly define "Uyghur," his analyses of related terms like "uy-" (to unite or adapt) and "ghur" (to unite or follow) inform modern interpretations.[3] Peter B. Golden, a historian specializing in Turkic studies, explains that "Uyghur" is traditionally interpreted as "united" or "allied," reflecting the confederation of various tribes. He derives the name from "uy-" (to unite) and "-ghur," indicating an agent, thus meaning "unifier" or "alliance maker."[4] Other interpretations suggest that "Uyghur" may have originally referred to a specific tribe within the Toquz Oghuz and was later adopted as the collective name for the confederation, with the term evolving to symbolize their identity as a culturally advanced people in Central Asia.[5]

Gathering of Uyghur Writers around the 1990s. Left to right: Turghun Almas (poet, historian), Imin Tursun (author, linguist), Abdurehim Otkur (author, poet), Mirsultan Osmanov (linguist), Hajinur Haji (author).

1.2.1 The 1921 Tashkent Conference and the Revival of Uyghur Identity

The 1921 Tashkent Conference was a pivotal moment when Uyghur scholars and intellectuals formally decided to revive the historical name "Uyghur" for their people, reconnecting them to the legacy of the Uyghur Khaganate and the Qocho Kingdom. Prior to this, for centuries, Uyghurs primarily identified their ethnicity as Turk or Turki, reflecting their linguistic and cultural ties to the broader Turkic world, as well as regional identities like Taranchi or Kashgari.^6 The adoption of "Uyghur" marked a deliberate effort to unify fragmented identities under a shared ethnical, historical, and cultural banner, symbolizing both pride in their past and a modern sense of national identity.^7

• •• • • • • • ••• • • • •• ••• • ••• •• • • ••• • •• •• •• •

Today, the majority of Uyghurs live in East Turkistan, XUAR or Xinjiang, which they consider their historical homeland. East Turkistan, located in northwestern China, is a vast, resource-rich region that borders several Central Asian countries. Outside China, sizable Uyghur diaspora communities exist in Kazakhstan, Kyrgyzstan, Uzbekistan, and Turkey, many of whom fled China during periods of political turmoil.

According to the Chinese government's census in 2020, the total population of East Turkistan was approximately 25.85 million.[7] Uyghurs accounted for 44.96% of the population (about 11.7 million), while Han Chinese represented 42.24%.[8] On the other hand, Uyghur advocacy groups and independent researchers have at times suggested that the Uyghur population may be undercounted or misrepresented in Chinese statistics, possibly due to internal migration policies, population control measures, or other factors.[9]

Before the Manchu Qing Empire's conquest and the incorporation of the Uyghur homeland, called Yette Sheher, in 1884, the region was predominantly inhabited by the Uyghurs and other Turkic groups such as Kazakhs and Kyrgyz, along with Mongolic groups like the Dzungars.[10] The Han Chinese population in East Turkistan was a very small minority.

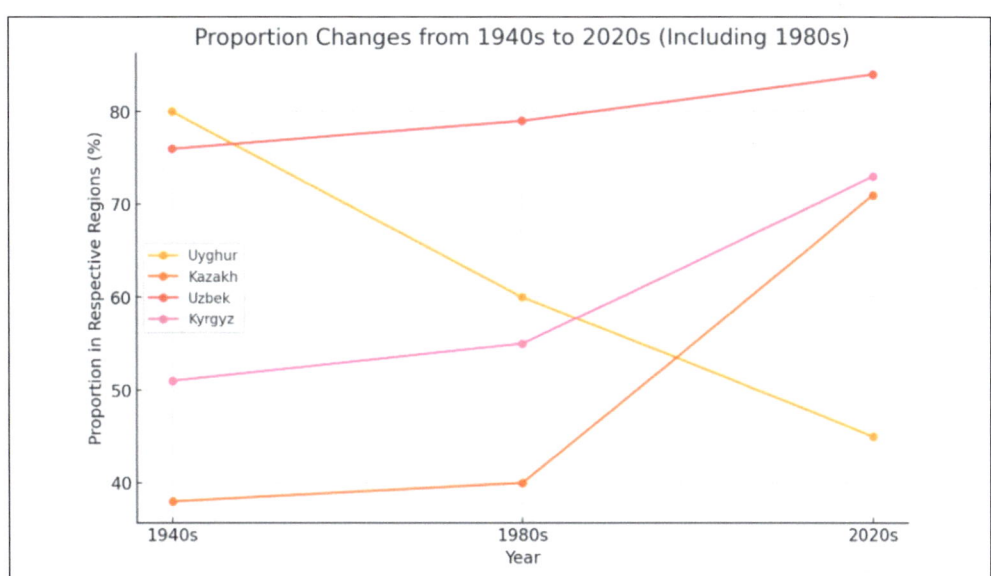

Uyghur population proportion in East Turkistan versus Kazakh in Kazakhstan, Uzbek in Uzbekistan, and Kyrgyz in Kyrgyzstan population proportion in their homeland.

In the 1940s, Uyghurs formed approximately 80% of East Turkistan's population, amounting to about 3 million people in a region of 3.73 million.[11] This demographic dominance began to shift after 1949, with the Chinese government implementing large-scale policies to encourage Han migration.[12] The demographic decline of Uyghurs relative to other groups can be directly attributed to mass Han Chinese migration policies, cultural assimilation campaigns, and human rights abuses, including mass detentions, forced labor, and reduced autonomy in reproductive health.[13], [14] Policies targeting

Uyghur language, religious practices, and cultural identity further suppressed their growth and influence within their historical homeland.[15, 16]

• ••   • • • • • • • • • •• • • •• • ••• ••

The Uyghur people speak the Uyghur language, a member of the southeastern Turkic language branch, closely related to Uzbek and other Turkic languages. Their identity is deeply connected to the ancient Turkic tribes that historically inhabited the steppes and oasis cities of Central Asia, with their presence in the region dating back thousands of years.[17]

Uyghur culture is a blend of Central Asian and Islamic influences. The Uyghurs traditionally practice Sunni Islam, which plays a central role in their identity. Before the mass surveillance and suppression campaigns by the Chinese government, Uyghurs maintained a rich religious and cultural life, with mosques and religious schools being focal points of Uyghur communities.[17, 18, 19]

• ••   • • • •• • • • ••• • •• • •••••• • • •• ••• • •• • • • •••• • • •• •••• • •• • • • • ••
    • • • • ••

The Uyghurs are widely recognized for their admirable qualities, deeply rooted in their rich cultural and spiritual traditions. Hospitality is one of their most celebrated traits, where welcoming guests is considered a profound duty and an expression of communal generosity. Whether hosting friends or strangers, Uyghur households traditionally prepare elaborate meals, showcasing their famed culinary artistry and warm, inclusive nature. This emphasis on fostering connections extends to their strong sense of community, where mutual support and collective well-being are central to daily life. Festivals, weddings, and shared labor in fields or businesses reflect a deep commitment to social cohesion, creating a vibrant cultural tapestry that values unity and collective progress. Resilience is another defining quality of the Uyghurs, demonstrated throughout their history of political upheavals and migrations. Despite these challenges, they have maintained their cultural identity, language, and traditions with remarkable strength. Their adaptability has also fueled entrepreneurial success, particularly in trade, where they historically thrived as key players along the Silk Road, connecting East and West.[20, 21]

• ••   • • • • • ••• ••• • •• •• • •

Introduction: The Uyghur People - Heritage, Struggle, and Legacy

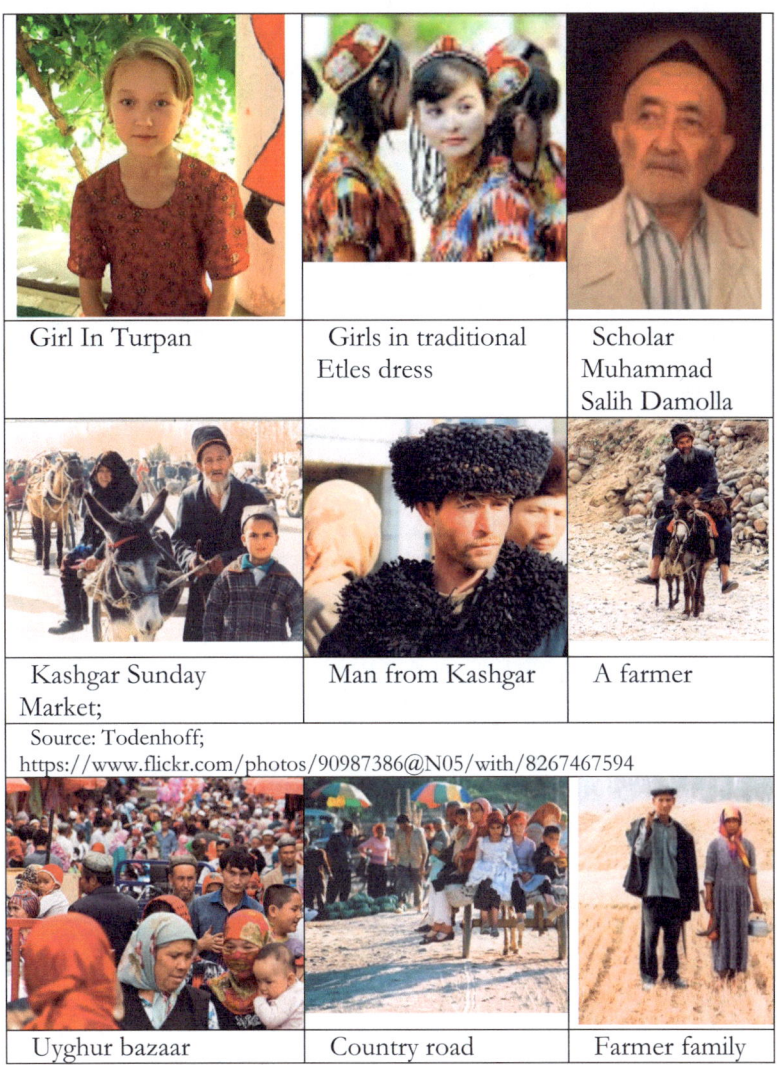

1.7.1 Cultural Intermediaries on the Silk Road

The Uyghurs played a key role in the Silk Road trade network, which connected China, Central Asia, and the Mediterranean. This trade route was not only a conduit for goods like silk, spices, and precious metals but also a channel for the exchange of ideas, religions, and technologies.^22

1.7.2 Development of Printing Technology

The Uyghurs are often credited as one of the first cultures to develop printing technology, centuries before printing spread in Europe. By the 8th and 9th centuries, the Uyghurs were using block printing techniques to produce religious texts and documents. This early form of printing allowed for the mass production of manuscripts, making Uyghur Buddhist, Manichaean, and later Islamic texts more accessible.^23 The discovery of printed Uyghur texts, alongside the well-known Chinese Diamond Sutra (868 CE), indicates that the Uyghurs were actively involved in printing technology around the same period as the Chinese.^24

1.7.3 Intellectual Contributions

Uyghur scholars like Mahmud al-Kashgari and Yusuf Has Hajib played pivotal roles in preserving and advancing Turkic and Islamic knowledge. Kashgari's *Diwan Lughat al-Turk* was the first comprehensive dictionary of Turkic languages, capturing not only linguistic information but also folklore and poetry.^25 His work helped bridge the cultural and linguistic gap between Turkic and Arab civilizations. His world map, created in the 11th century, is a remarkable representation of the Turkic world, reflecting the geographical knowledge and cultural significance of the era. Similarly, Yusuf Has Hajib's *Kutadgu Bilig* is an important political treatise that combined Islamic principles with Turkic wisdom, offering guidance on governance and justice.^26

1.7.4 Influence on the Mongol Empire

When the Mongol emperor Genghis Khan conquered the Uyghur Kingdom of Qocho in the early 13th century, he recognized the advanced culture, literacy, and administrative expertise of the Uyghurs. Instead of destroying their institutions, Genghis Khan incorporated Uyghur officials into his administration. The Uyghurs introduced the Uyghur script, which became the official writing system of the Mongol Empire.^27 Their bureaucratic expertise helped the Mongols administer their vast empire, which spanned much of Asia and Europe.

The Uyghur contribution to Mongol governance helped ensure the efficiency and stability of one of the largest empires in history. The Ottoman Sultan Mehmed II even had Uyghur script taught in his court, and one of his documents, the "Victory Letter of Otlukbeli," was written in Uyghur script and Eastern Turkic (closely related to the Uyghur language). This document, composed by Sheyhzade Abdurrezak Bahshı on August 30, 1473, was addressed to the Turkomans of Anatolia.^28

1.7.5 Scientific and Architectural Achievements

The Karez underground irrigation system, extensively utilized in Turpan, is a testament to their engineering prowess.^29 Their contributions to medicine, including early surgical techniques, further emphasize their role as custodians of scientific knowledge along the Silk Road.^30

In conclusion, the Uyghurs and their ancestors made lasting contributions to global civilization through their intellectual, cultural, and technological innovations. Their strategic role in the exchange of knowledge along the Silk Road, their pioneering work in printing, and their influence on the Mongol Empire and Islamic world highlight their important legacy. Uyghur culture also includes a rich tradition of music, dance, and literature. The muqam, a form of classical Uyghur music, is a UNESCO-recognized cultural heritage.^31

Notes

1. Sean R. Roberts, *The War on the Uyghurs: China's Internal Campaign Against a Muslim Minority* (Princeton, NJ: Princeton University Press, 2020).
2. Amy K. Lehr, "Addressing Forced Labor in the Xinjiang Uyghur Autonomous Region," Center for Strategic and International Studies, 2020.
3. Mahmud al-Kashgari, *Dīwān Lughāt al-Turk*, 11th century.
4. Peter B. Golden, *An Introduction to the History of the Turkic Peoples* (Wiesbaden: Harrassowitz Verlag, 1992).
5. Gerard Clauson, *An Etymological Dictionary of Pre-Thirteenth-Century Turkish* (Oxford: Clarendon Press, 1972).
6. Linda Benson, *The Ili Rebellion: The Moslem Challenge to Chinese Authority in Xinjiang, 1944–1949* (Armonk, NY: M.E. Sharpe, 1990).
7. Michal Biran, *The Empire of the Qara Khitai in Eurasian History* (Cambridge: Cambridge University Press, 2005).
8. "Gov.cn," accessed December 19, 2024.
9. Adrian Zenz, "Sterilizations, IUDs, and Mandatory Birth Control: The CCP's Campaign to Suppress Uyghur Birthrates in Xinjiang," *Journal of Political Risk* 7, no. 7 (2019).
10. Stanley W. Toops, "The Demography of Xinjiang," in *Xinjiang: China's Muslim Borderland*, ed. S. Frederick Starr (Armonk, NY: M.E. Sharpe, 2004).
11. Ibid.
12. Roberts, *The War on the Uyghurs*.
13. Zenz, "Sterilizations, IUDs, and Mandatory Birth Control."
14. Timothy A. Grose, *Negotiating Inseparability in China: The Xinjiang Class and the Dynamics of Uyghur Identity* (Hong Kong: Hong Kong University Press, 2020).

15. Adrian Zenz and James Leibold, "Xinjiang's Rapid Demographic Shift: Causes, Consequences, and Implications," *China Brief* 20, no. 10 (2020): 5–9.
16. Human Rights Watch, "China's Repression of Uyghurs in Xinjiang," accessed December 19, 2024, https://www.hrw.org.
17. Colin Mackerras, *The Uygur Empire According to the T'ang Dynastic Histories* (Canberra: Australian National University Press, 1972).
18. Rachel Harris, *Soundscapes of Uyghur Islam* (Bloomington: Indiana University Press, 2020).
19. Darren Byler, "The Global Implications of 'Re-education' Technologies in Northwest China," *ChinaFile* (2019).
20. Rahile Dawut, "Shrine Pilgrimage and Uyghur Identity," *The Silk Road* 3, no. 1 (2005): 2–7.
21. Joanne N. Smith Finley, *The Art of Symbolic Resistance: Uyghur Identities and Uyghur-Han Relations in Contemporary Xinjiang* (Leiden: Brill, 2013).
22. Thomas T. Allsen, *Culture and Conquest in Mongol Eurasia* (Cambridge: Cambridge University Press, 2001).
23. Valerie Hansen, *The Silk Road: A New History* (Oxford: Oxford University Press, 2012).
24. Christoph Baumer, *The History of Central Asia: The Age of the Silk Roads* (London: I.B.Tauris, 2014).
25. Mahmud al-Kashgari, *Dīwān Lughāt al-Turk*, 11th century.
26. Peter B. Golden, *An Introduction to the History of the Turkic Peoples* (Wiesbaden: Harrassowitz Verlag, 1992), 340.
27. Colin Mackerras, *The Uygur Empire According to the T'ang Dynastic Histories* (Canberra: Australian National University Press, 1972), 87.
28. Linda Benson, *The Ili Rebellion: The Moslem Challenge to Chinese Authority in Xinjiang, 1944–1949* (Armonk, NY: M.E. Sharpe, 1990), 142.
29. Abudu, Shalamu, Sevinc Yeliz Cevik, Salim Bawazir, and James P. King. "Vitality of Ancient Karez Systems in Arid Lands." *Water History* 3, no. 3 (2011): 213–25. https://doi.org/10.1007/s12685-011-0044-5.
30. Wusiman, Abula, Shayibuzhati M., and Zhang X. "Traditional Uyghur Medicine: Historical Perspective and Modern Practice." *Alternative Therapies in Health and Medicine* 23, no. 6 (2017): 34–41.
31. UNESCO, "The Muqam of the Uyghurs," accessed December 19, 2024, https://www.unesco.org

Origins and Ancestry

The Uyghurs are part of a larger Turkic ethno-linguistic group with origins in the Eurasian steppes. Scholars believe that the Turkic peoples, including the Uyghurs, trace their ancestry to ancient nomadic tribes such as the Xiongnu (Huns) and were influenced by earlier groups like the Saka, whose cultural and genetic legacy shaped the Central Asian region. The Saka, a nomadic group associated with the Scythians, were known for their warrior culture and elaborate burial mounds, contributing to the cultural development of Turkic societies. Archaeological evidence, such as the Pazyryk burial mounds in the Altai Mountains, highlights the Saka's influence in the steppe regions.^32 The Huns, another notable group emerging from Central Asia, were recognized for their military prowess and significant influence on both the Eastern and Western Roman Empires. Their migration into Europe shaped the ethnic and cultural dynamics of Eurasia.^33

Geographical Distribution of Uyghur Ancestors and Related Nomadic Tribes in 200 BC. Author: Thomas A. Lessman. Source https://www.worldhistorymaps.info/ancient/200-bc/

According to ancient Chinese historical texts, such as the *Book of Wei*, the *Zhoushu* (Book of Zhou), and the *Suishu* (Book of Sui), the Uyghurs trace their origins to the Tiele tribes, a Turkic confederation that emerged after the disintegration of the Xiongnu (Hun) confederacy. The Tiele are often regarded as the cultural, political, and genetic successors of the Xiongnu, inheriting their steppe traditions and tribal confederation model. The continuity between these groups is evident, as many tribal names and regions mentioned in Xiongnu records later appear in association with the Tiele. The Tiele confederation included diverse groups that played a critical role in the development of Turkic identities and the eventual rise of the Uyghurs as a distinct power in Central Asia.^34 While the Uyghurs have historical connections to these ancient groups, numerous contemporary Western scholars argue that modern Uyghurs are not direct linear descendants of the Uyghur Khaganate in Mongolia. Instead, they view the modern Uyghurs as descendants of multiple groups, one of which includes the ancient Uyghurs.^35

Additionally, the cultural and genetic diversity of the Uyghur population has been influenced by other groups, such as the Tocharians. The Tocharians, an Indo-European people who inhabited the Tarim Basin (modern East Turkistan), interacted with Turkic populations, further enriching the cultural heritage of the region.^36

Notes

32. Nicola Di Cosmo, *Ancient China and Its Enemies: The Rise of Nomadic Power in East Asian History* (Cambridge: Cambridge University Press, 2002), 156.
33. Christopher I. Beckwith, *Empires of the Silk Road: A History of Central Eurasia from the Bronze Age to the Present* (Princeton, NJ: Princeton University Press, 2009), 119.
34. *Book of Wei (Wei Shu)*, compiled in the 6th century.
35. James A. Millward, *Eurasian Crossroads: A History of Xinjiang* (New York: Columbia University Press, 2007), 35; Millward and Perdue, "Political and Cultural History of Xinjiang," in *The Chinese State at the Borders*, ed. Thomas J. Barfield (Cambridge: Harvard University Press, 2004), 87; Susan Henders, *Negotiating Nationalism: Nation-Building, Federalism, and Secession in the Multinational State* (Oxford: Oxford University Press, 2006), 50.
36. Victor H. Mair, "The Tarim Mummies and Their Indo-European Connections," in *The Tarim Mummies: Ancient China and the Mystery of the Earliest Peoples from the West*, ed. J. P. Mallory and Victor H. Mair (London: Thames & Hudson, 2000), 240.

In ancient times, the modern region known as East Turkistan or the Xinjiang Uyghur Autonomous Region was referenced by various civilizations, including the Romans, Persians, Armenians, and Chinese. These accounts provide valuable insights into the region's historical significance as a cultural and trade crossroads.

Herodotus, the Greek historian of the 5th century BCE, mentioned the Scythians, nomadic tribes who occupied areas that included modern-day East Turkistan. These tribes were known for their equestrian skills and warrior culture, as described in *The Histories*.^37 During the Sasanian era, interactions with Central Asian tribes reflected the region's role as a pivotal cultural and trade crossroads, further cementing its historical significance.^38

Pliny the Elder, writing in the 1st century CE, referred to the "Seres" in his work *Natural History*. These people were linked to the silk-producing cultures of Central Asia, indirectly associating East Turkistan with vital trade centers along the Silk Road.^39 In the 2nd century CE, Ptolemy described regions beyond the Pamirs in his *Geographia*, including a location called "Kasia," which is identified with Kashgar. He noted the people of this area as tall and robust, with some possessing green or light eyes.^40 Ptolemy further described the people of Serica as "*exceeding the ordinary human height, with flaxen hair and blue eyes.*"^41

Ptolomy's book described people in Serica as "exceeded the ordinary human height, had flaxen hair, and blue eyes".

• •• • •• • • • • • • • • •

Sima Qian (2nd century BCE), in *Records of the Grand Historian*, documented interactions with nomadic tribes in western regions, mentioning key cities like Kashgar and Khotan.^42

• •• •• • • • • • • •• •••• • • •• •• •

The term Turkistan first appeared in historical records during the Abbasid Caliphate around the 8th century. It was noted by the Persian geographer Ibn Khordadbeh in his *Book of Roads and Kingdoms (Kitāb al-Masālik wa'l-Mamālik)*.^43 The term Turkistan was

13

broadly used by Arab and Persian geographers to describe lands inhabited by Turkic peoples east of the Oxus River (Amu Darya), covering much of Central Asia. Derived from the Persian suffix "-stan," meaning "land of," Turkistan referred to regions with established Turkic populations.[44]

Historically, Turkistan described a vast area, including parts of modern-day Kazakhstan, Uzbekistan, Turkmenistan, Kyrgyzstan, and East Turkistan. It symbolized regions where Turkic culture and influence flourished, with East Turkistan playing a key role as a cultural and historical center of this expansive geography.

Notes

37. Herodotus, *The Histories*, trans. Aubrey de Sélincourt (Harmondsworth: Penguin Books, 1954), 200.
38. Touraj Daryaee, *Sasanian Persia: The Rise and Fall of an Empire* (London: I.B. Tauris, 2009), 130.
39. Pliny the Elder, *Natural History*, trans. H. Rackham (Cambridge: Harvard University Press, 1938), 6.26.
40. Ptolemy, *Geographia*, trans. Edward Luther Stevenson (New York: Cosimo Classics, 2014), Book 6, Chapter 16.
41. Ibid., Book 6, Chapter 17.
42. Sima Qian, *Records of the Grand Historian*, trans. Burton Watson (New York: Columbia University Press, 1993), 128–130.
43. Ibn Khordadbeh, *Book of Roads and Kingdoms*, trans. Guy Le Strange (Cambridge: Cambridge University Press, 1889), 42.
44. Christopher I. Beckwith, *Empires of the Silk Road: A History of Central Eurasia from the Bronze Age to the Present* (Princeton, NJ: Princeton University Press, 2009), 250.

The question of whether modern Uyghurs are Uyghurs or Turks reflects a complex mix of historical, linguistic, and cultural dimensions of identity. This discussion is rooted in the rich history of the Uyghur people, their Turkic origins, and their development as a distinct group in Central Asia. To understand this identity, we can explore several perspectives that clarify why Uyghurs are often seen as both Uyghur and Turk, and why they are considered among the original Turkic peoples.

The name "Uyghur" evolved significantly over the centuries, transitioning from a tribal designation within Turkic alliances to a distinct ethnic identity. Originally, the Uyghurs were part of the Tiele confederation, a coalition of nomadic Turkic tribes in the 5th and 6th centuries CE, where they began to emerge as a prominent group known for their leadership and resilience.^45 During the Gokturk period, the Uyghurs were also part of the Toquz Oghuz ("Nine Oghuz") confederation, an alliance of nine Turkic tribes. This confederation strengthened the Uyghurs' status among the Turkic peoples, allowing them to organize politically and militarily.^46 At this stage, "Uyghur" primarily represented a tribal identity within a larger Turkic context.^47

Following the collapse of the Gokturk Khaganate, the Uyghurs rose to power and established the Uyghur Khaganate in 744 CE. This marked a transformation from a tribal designation to an imperial identity, as the Uyghur Khaganate extended its influence across Central Asia, ruling over various Turkic and non-Turkic groups. The Uyghur name then became synonymous with the ruling elite of the empire, spreading to encompass their subjects and solidifying as a broader identity.^48

When the Uyghur Khaganate fell in 840 CE due to Kyrgyz invasions, Uyghurs under the leadership of remaining aristocrats migrated southwest to the Tarim Basin and established the Qocho Kingdom near Turpan.^49 Here, the Uyghur name became a symbol of their imperial heritage. Over time, the residents of the Qocho Kingdom, regardless of their specific tribal origins, began identifying as Uyghur, thus transforming "Uyghur" from a tribal or imperial label into a regional and ethnic identity.^50 This identity persisted well beyond the kingdom's decline, as the Uyghurs continued to inhabit the Tarim Basin and maintain their cultural traditions.

Throughout their history, Uyghur elites and ruling classes often referred to themselves as "Turks" or "Turki," emphasizing their Turkic heritage. The rulers of the Uyghur Khaganate (744–840 CE) strongly embraced this Turkic identity, fostering a shared cultural and linguistic tradition.^51 This legacy was carried forward by the Karakhanids (840–1212 CE), the first Islamic Turkic Khaganate, which upheld and enriched Turkic traditions.^52 Mahmud al-Kashgari, in his *Dīwān Lughāt al-Turk*, celebrated the Turkic language and culture, reflecting the enduring influence of this heritage.^53 Similarly, while the founders of the Yarkent Khanate (1514–1705 CE) had Mongol roots, the ruling elite and the predominantly Turkic population of the khanate had, by that time, fully adopted Turkic identity, language, and culture, shaped by the region's demographic and cultural dynamics.^54 Collectively, these khanates preserved and promoted a unified Turkic cultural legacy across Central Asia, further solidifying the Uyghur identity as an integral part of the larger Turkic world.

• •• • • • • • • •• • •• • • • •• •••• • •• • ••• •• • ••• • • • •• •• • • • •• •

The Uyghurs are widely regarded as one of the original Turkic peoples due to their early establishment of a Turkic state and contributions to Turkic culture. The Uyghur Khaganate and the Karakhanid Empire were foundational to the Turkic world,^55 with Kashgar as a cultural and intellectual center, alongside cities like Qocho (Turpan), Khotan, and Yarkent, which fostered advancements in Turkic language, literature, and religion.^56 This historical continuity has helped preserve Turkic language, literature, and customs, positioning the Uyghurs as early pioneers in Turkic civilization.

• •• • • ••• •• ••• • • •• •• • • •• ••• •• • • • • • ••• •

Culturally and linguistically, Uyghurs are an integral part of the Turkic family. The Uyghur language, closely related to Uzbek, belongs to the Turkic language group and reflects shared linguistic roots with other Central Asian Turkic languages.^57 Islam, which became dominant in Uyghur society after the 10th century, and centuries of exchange with other Turkic, Persian, and Chinese cultures have further enriched Uyghur identity.^58

However, Uyghurs have also developed a distinct cultural heritage, shaped by their specific history in the Tarim Basin. Their unique customs, music, and traditions distinguish them from other Turkic groups like the Kazakhs, Kyrgyz, and others. Thus, while culturally Turkic, the Uyghurs possess a distinct identity that sets them apart.^58

Modern Uyghurs identify primarily as Uyghur, a term that reflects their specific ethnic, cultural, and historical experiences. Although ethnically Turkic, Uyghurs see themselves as a distinct group with an identity rooted in their historical homeland in East Turkistan.^58 This unique identity is often emphasized over a broader Turkic label, even as they share ancestry and language with other Turkic peoples.

In summary, modern Uyghurs embody both Uyghur and Turkic identities. Historically and linguistically, they are Turkic, descending from ancient Turkic tribes and speaking a Turkic language. However, their ethnic identity is uniquely Uyghur, shaped by a distinct cultural heritage and historical legacy. As part of the larger Turkic world, Uyghurs have developed a unique identity that highlights their contributions as one of the original Turkic peoples, rooted in a region they have called home for centuries.

Thus, modern Uyghurs can be seen as both **Uyghurs** and **Turks**. They are **Uyghur** in the sense that they have a distinct ethnic identity tied to their unique history and culture, but they are also **Turkic** in their language, genetic ancestry, and broader cultural connections.

Notes

45. Colin Mackerras, *The Uygur Empire According to the T'ang Dynastic Histories* (Canberra: Australian National University Press, 1972), 87.
46. James A. Millward, *Eurasian Crossroads: A History of Xinjiang* (New York: Columbia University Press, 2007), 41.
47. Christopher I. Beckwith, *Empires of the Silk Road: A History of Central Eurasia from the Bronze Age to the Present* (Princeton, NJ: Princeton University Press, 2009), 119.
48. Ibid., 130.
49. Linda Benson, *China's Last Nomads: The History and Culture of China's Kazakhs* (Armonk, NY: M.E. Sharpe, 1998), 72.
50. Mackerras, *The Uygur Empire According to the T'ang Dynastic Histories*, 99.
51. Lars Johanson, *Turkic: An International Handbook* (Berlin: De Gruyter Mouton, 2010), 128.
52. Joanne N. Smith Finley, *The Art of Symbolic Resistance: Uyghur Identities and Uyghur-Han Relations in Contemporary Xinjiang* (Leiden: Brill, 2013), 182.
53. Millward, *Eurasian Crossroads*, 44.
54. Colin Mackerras, *The Uygur Empire According to the T'ang Dynastic Histories*, 120.
55. Christoph Baumer, *The History of Central Asia: The Age of the Steppe Warriors* (London: I.B. Tauris, 2012), 199.
56. Lars Johanson, *Turkic: An International Handbook* (Berlin: De Gruyter Mouton, 2010), 128.

57. Joanne N. Smith Finley, *The Art of Symbolic Resistance: Uyghur Identities and Uyghur-Han Relations in Contemporary Xinjiang* (Leiden: Brill, 2013), 182.
58. Millward, *Eurasian Crossroads*, 44.

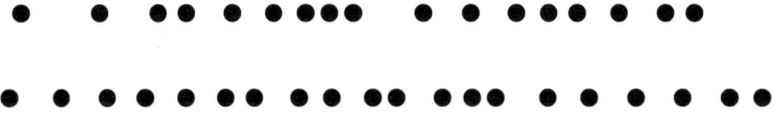

5.1.1 The Lost Tocharians: Tracing the Indo-European Roots and Legacy in the Uyghur Heartland

The Tocharians were an ancient Indo-European people who inhabited the Tarim Basin in what is now East Turkistan, beginning around the second millennium BCE. They are believed to have migrated eastward from the western steppe regions, likely as part of early Indo-European movements across Central Asia. Archaeological evidence, including distinctive mummies with European-like features and elaborate textiles, reveals that they created a culturally rich civilization in the desert oases of the Tarim Basin. Their strategic location connected them to the broader Silk Road, facilitating significant cultural exchanges between East and West.^59

5.1.2 Linguistic Connections

Tocharian, a branch of the Indo-European language family, includes two main dialects: Tocharian A and Tocharian B. The language shares roots with other Indo-European languages, such as Sanskrit, Greek, and Latin. This classification suggests an early migration eastward, isolating the Tocharians from other Indo-European developments and preserving a unique linguistic identity.^60 Despite their prolonged presence in Central Asia, Tocharian remained distinct from other regional languages, likely due to the Tocharians' cultural isolation.^61

5.1.3 Merging with the Uyghurs

It is a well-regarded but hypothetical view that the complete merging of the Tocharians with Turkic groups culminated in the 9th century CE.^61 After the fall of the Uyghur Khaganate in Mongolia in 840 CE, many Uyghurs migrated into the Tarim Basin, eventually settling there and establishing the Kingdom of Qocho near Turpan. This influx introduced a substantial Turkic presence into the region, where they encountered the remaining Tocharian population. Hypothetically, the Uyghurs, with their Turkic language and customs, integrated the Tocharians through cultural assimilation, intermarriage, and shared practices.^62 Buddhism, practiced by both Tocharians and Uyghurs, may have served as a cultural bridge that eased this integration.^63

As Uyghur influence expanded over the Tarim Basin, it is assumed that the Tocharian language and identity gradually faded, replaced by the Uyghurs' Turkic language and cultural norms. Over generations, it is thought that the Tocharians became fully absorbed into Uyghur society, contributing to the Uyghur cultural mosaic and potentially adding unique elements to Uyghur art, physical diversity, and certain religious traditions.^64

5.1.4 Legacy of the Tocharians

Although the Tocharians no longer exist as a distinct ethnic group, their legacy endures in Central Asia's historical and cultural landscape. Discoveries of Tocharian manuscripts, mummies, and artifacts in East Turkistan have provided valuable insights into the early civilizations of the Tarim Basin and Indo-European migrations. These findings underscore the Tocharians' role as a cultural bridge on the Silk Road, contributing to the blending of Eastern and Western traditions.^65 While the Tocharians as a people disappeared, their influence persists in the Uyghur people, who exemplify the region's layered history of migration, cultural convergence, and enduring heritage.^65

5.2.1 The Saka-Scythians: Nomadic Architects of Central Asian Heritage

The Saka, a branch of the Scythians, were nomadic peoples who inhabited the vast territories of the Eurasian steppes, stretching from the Black Sea region (modern Ukraine and southern Russia) in the west to Central Asia, including present-day Kazakhstan, Uzbekistan, and East Turkistan, in the east.^66 Their presence spanned regions critical to ancient trade and cultural exchange, linking Europe, the Middle East, and Asia.^67

The Saka roamed the steppes of Central Asia and the region now known as East Turkistan from the 1st millennium BCE. Recognized for their exceptional skills in horseback riding, archery, and metalwork, the Saka left an indelible mark on the history and culture of the Eurasian steppe.^68 Their influence extended across early trade networks and cultural exchanges, playing a critical role in the development of what would later become the Silk Road.^69

The Saka were ancient nomadic peoples of the Central Asian steppes, known for their warrior culture, long hair, intricate craftsmanship, and skillful horseback riding.

Culturally and genetically, the Saka contributed significantly to the foundations of many Central Asian societies, especially the Turkic peoples, including the Uyghurs who emerged in later centuries.^70 The Saka not only passed down warrior traditions but also shaped linguistic, social, and political structures in the region.^70 Additionally, related groups such as the Massagetae, Issedones, and the Yuezhi shared elements of the Saka-Scythian heritage, establishing interconnected communities that bolstered trade, alliances, and cultural exchange.^71

The nomads' impact is evident in the artifacts and burial sites that survive today, which highlight a dynamic, skilled society whose legacy continued to shape Central Asia for centuries. The Saka not only laid the groundwork for the region's cultural and ethnic diversity but also influenced empires, from the Parthians to the Kushans, establishing them as enduring figures in the heritage of the Eurasian steppe.[71]

Notes

59. Victor H. Mair and J. P. Mallory, *The Tarim Mummies: Ancient China and the Mystery of the Earliest Peoples from the West* (London: Thames & Hudson, 2000), 120.
60. Douglas Q. Adams, "Tocharian Languages," in *Encyclopedia of Indo-European Culture*, ed. James P. Mallory and Douglas Q. Adams (London: Fitzroy Dearborn, 1997), 597.
61. Peter B. Golden, *An Introduction to the History of the Turkic Peoples* (Wiesbaden: Harrassowitz Verlag, 1992), 154.
62. Valerie Hansen, *The Silk Road: A New History with Documents* (New York: Oxford University Press, 2012), 54.
63. Christoph Baumer, *The History of Central Asia: The Age of the Steppe Warriors* (London: I.B. Tauris, 2012), 98.
64. Ibid., 99.
65. Ibid., 100.
66. Barry Cunliffe, *The Scythians: Nomad Warriors of the Steppe* (Oxford: Oxford University Press, 2019), 87.
67. Christopher I. Beckwith, *Empires of the Silk Road: A History of Central Eurasia from the Bronze Age to the Present* (Princeton, NJ: Princeton University Press, 2009), 120.
68. M. G. Moshkova, *The Steppe and the Sown* (Cambridge: Cambridge University Press, 1996), 89.
69. Beckwith, *Empires of the Silk Road*, 122.
70. Nicola Di Cosmo, *Ancient China and Its Enemies: The Rise of Nomadic Power in East Asian History* (Cambridge: Cambridge University Press, 2004), 146.
71. Baumer, *The History of Central Asia: The Age of the Steppe Warriors*, 211.

From Empires to Exile: A Brief Uyghur History

The question of Uyghur indigeneity in East Turkistan is supported by significant historical, linguistic, and genetic evidence that reflects a continuity of culture and heritage over millennia. While tracing direct lineage to ancient populations such as the Saka or Tocharians is complex, historical records, linguistic connections, and recent genetic research make a compelling case for Uyghurs as indigenous to the region.

East Turkistan has long been a cultural crossroads, inhabited by ancient peoples like the Saka (Scythians) and Tocharians.^73 Some Uyghur and Turkic scholars propose that these early inhabitants may have had Turkic roots or strong connections with early Turkic groups, blending influences across the region. Roman and Chinese sources describe the Saka as nomadic, warrior-like people, similar to the Turkic tribes that later thrived in Central Asia, suggesting a possible ancestral or cultural link between proto-Turkic peoples and the region.^72 Classical historians, including Roman and Byzantine scholars, often referred to Turkic groups such as the Huns and Göktürks as "Scythians," indicating a perceived continuity between these nomadic cultures.^73 Persian historical sources, such as Zubdat al-Tawarikh by Hafiz-i Abru, associate the Karakhanids with the legendary figure Afrasiab, reinforcing a deep-rooted Turkic presence in Central Asia and East Turkistan.^74

While the Tocharians and Saka thrived in the Tarim Basin, Turkic-speaking groups were present in the broader Central Asian region, particularly from the 1st millennium CE. Proto-Turkic groups, possibly including ancestors of the Huns, likely influenced various cultures across the steppes.^75

The Ashina clan, founders of the Göktürk Khaganate, played a pivotal role in Turkic state formation and are believed to have originated from regions encompassing present-day East Turkistan. Their ruling dynasty is linked to the Khotanese Saka language, with scholars such as András Róna-Tas proposing that the name "Ashina" may derive from the

23

Khotanese Saka term "āššIna," meaning "deep blue."^76 Similarly, the ethnonym "Turk" is suggested to originate from the Khotanese Saka word "tturakä," meaning "lid" or "helmet," which aligns with Chinese historical accounts describing the term's association with a mountain's helmet-like shape.^77 The earliest known written mention of the term "Türük" (tturuk) appears in a Khotanese Saka text from the 4th-5th centuries CE, predating the Orkhon Inscriptions and indicating early Turkic presence or influence in the region.

The timeline for the adoption of these terms is not precisely defined. However, the Göktürks, led by the Ashina clan, rose to prominence in the 6th century CE, indicating these names were in use by that time. The Khotanese Saka language, spoken in the Kingdom of Khotan during the first millennium CE, suggests long-term interaction between the native Saka inhabitants and Ashina-led Turkic groups.

The Saka were present in the region from the 1st millennium BCE, and their language and traditions persisted until at least the 10th century CE, overlapping with the emergence of the Proto-Turks. The intermingling of the Saka (an Indo-European group) with Turkic steppe nomads likely contributed to the early ethnogenesis of the Turkic identity, with the Ashina clan possibly emerging from this complex cultural landscape.

The connection between East Turkistan and Turkic origins became more evident with the rise of the Göktürk Khaganate in the 6th century CE, when Turkic tribes, including the Göktürks, expanded into Central Asia.^78 Chinese historical texts, such as the Zhou Shu and Sui Shu, trace the Göktürks' lineage to the Altai Mountains and surrounding areas in modern East Turkistan and Mongolia. The Ashina clan is also linked to East Turkistan through their wolf origin legend as recorded in Chinese annals like the Zhou Shu and Bei Shi. The narrative describes their refuge in a remote area characterized as a cave or valley surrounded by high mountains, situated "north of Gaochang"—modern-day Uyghur city Turpan.^78

Sources such as The Cambridge History of Early Inner Asia provide evidence supporting this connection through historical records of the Göktürks' migration and their governance over East Turkistan. This deep historical connection underscores East Turkistan's role as a central locus of Turkic cultural and political identity. The Turks in World History further emphasizes East Turkistan's role as a cradle of Turkic civilization, underlining its significance in early Turkic migrations and state-building.^79 These records illustrate East Turkistan as more than a geographic region; it represents the heart of an evolving Turkic heritage.

The 8th-century emergence of the Uyghur Khaganate continued this Turkic influence.^80 Following its collapse, the Uyghurs migrated southwest to East Turkistan, forming states such as the Qocho Kingdom and the Karakhanid Khaganate. This migration was not into foreign territory but into a region rich with Turkic history. The presence of earlier Turkic groups such as the Huns, White Huns (Hephthalites), Tiele, and Göktürks in East Turkistan supports the view that modern Uyghurs are both descendants of these early Turkic peoples and later arrivals following the fall of the Uyghur Khaganate.^81

• •• • • • • ••• •• • •• • • • • • • • • •••• • ••• • • •• • • • • • • •• •• •• •

Recent genetic studies further corroborate the Uyghur indigeneity in East Turkistan. A 2008 study published in the American Journal of Human Genetics by Shuhua Xu et al. examined the Uyghur population and identified it as a quintessential example of admixture between Eastern and Western anthropometric traits. By analyzing over 20,000 single nucleotide polymorphisms (SNPs)—variations at a single position in DNA sequences across chromosome 21—the researchers concluded that the Uyghur genetic profile represents a two-way admixture, approximately 60% European and 40% East Asian, estimated to have occurred around 2,520 years ago,^82 substantiating the historical presence of modern Uyghur ancestors in East Turkistan long before the fall of the Uyghur Khaganate in 840 CE, a pivotal event that shaped the region's political and cultural landscape. Furthermore, this evidence challenges the prevailing belief that the modern Uyghur population arose solely from the mixture of the Caucasoid native inhabitants of ancient East Turkistan and the Turkic Uyghurs who migrated from Mongolia.

The presence of paternal haplogroups among Uyghurs, such as R1a (linked to European and South/Central Asian origins) and Q (found in Native American, Central Asian, and Siberian populations), suggests genetic continuity with ancient inhabitants, like the Saka.^83 Victor H. Mair and J. P. Mallory discuss how findings from Tarim Basin mummies confirm the existence of populations with physical and genetic traits linked to both Western and Eastern origins, reflecting the complex ancestry of modern Uyghurs.^80 This genetic evidence strengthens the case for population continuity and highlights the region's deep history of interaction and integration.

• •• • • ••• •• ••• • • • • • • • • • • ••• • •• • • • •• ••• • •• •• •• •••• • ••• • •

The diverse ancestry of the Uyghur people reflects influences from various civilizations that have shaped the region over millennia. The Tocharians, an Indo-European group known for their distinct cultural artifacts and linguistic uniqueness, inhabited the Tarim Basin and played a crucial role in the cultural history of East Turkistan. Their interactions influenced early religious, artistic, and economic developments in East Turkistan, establishing the region as a center of cross-cultural connectivity.^85

Similarly, the Saka's warrior culture and steppe lifestyle played a critical role in shaping the Turkic identity, particularly through their interactions with the Ashina-led Turkic groups. The prolonged coexistence of the Saka and early Turkic-speaking populations in East Turkistan facilitated extensive cultural and linguistic exchanges. These exchanges contributed to the formation of distinct Turkic governance structures, military strategies, and social customs, elements later solidified under Ashina rule. Today, Uyghur cultural identity reflects these deep historical layers, from traditional Uyghur art to horsemanship traditions that mark Turkic heritage.^86

The legacy of the Tocharians and Saka-Scythians endures in Uyghur identity, particularly through cultural and linguistic preservation. Place names like Oghuzsak, Toqquzsak, and Ikkisak retain the ancient "Sak" designation, serving as markers of the region's layered heritage and the synthesis of Indo-European and Turkic influences.

• •• • • • •• • •• •• • • • • • • • ••• • • •• • • •• • • • • • •••• • •• • • • •••

Ablet Kamalov, a historian from Kazakhstan, and Ablet Khojaev, a historian from Uzbekistan, present complementary arguments affirming the Uyghurs' indigeneity in East Turkistan.^87 Kamalov emphasizes the Uyghurs' deep-rooted presence by tracing their origins to interactions between Indo-European groups such as the Tocharians and Saka and Turkic-speaking nomads like the Xiongnu and Tiele, highlighting the continuity of populations in the region.

Similarly, Khojaev underscores the Uyghurs' over 2,000-year presence in East Turkistan, tracing their lineage to ancient groups like the Yuezhi and Xiongnu and linking them to entities such as the Uyghur Khaganate and Qocho Uyghur Kingdom. Drawing on Chinese sources, archaeological evidence from the Tarim Basin, and genetic analysis, Khojaev further reinforces the argument for population continuity, challenging narratives that question Uyghur indigeneity^88. Together, these scholars provide a robust case for the Uyghurs' enduring connection to East Turkistan, rooted in both historical and genetic evidence.

• •• • •• •• • ••• • ••• • • • • • • ••• • •• • • •• • • •••• • ••

The Uyghurs' historical connection to East Turkistan is more than a matter of lineage; it represents a profound cultural and spiritual bond. Uyghur identity has been shaped by empires, cultural exchanges, and continuous adaptation to Central Asia's shifting political landscapes. From the ancient mummies of the Tarim Basin to the carved inscriptions of the Uyghur Khaganate, each historical layer reveals a resilient heritage that has endured through time.

Key Uyghur cities such as Kashgar, Khotan, and Turpan—along with Urumchi, which is located near the ancient Uyghur city of Beshbaliq, a key center of the Qocho Uyghur Kingdom—have been inhabited for thousands of years, serving as cultural, religious, and economic hubs along the Silk Road. Archaeological discoveries from the Tarim Basin, including the Kiroran (Loulan), Cherchen, and Small River Cemetery (Ördek's Necropolis/Xiaohe) mummies, provide evidence of the region's ancient inhabitants, whose descendants still walk these lands today. The very same landscapes where the Saka, Tocharians, and early Turkic peoples once thrived continue to be home to the Uyghurs, underscoring their enduring connection to East Turkistan.

Thus, the Uyghur story transcends territorial roots, reflecting the enduring strength of a people deeply connected to their homeland. Their history defies a singular narrative, embodying the adaptability and continuity of a civilization both shaped by and shaping East Turkistan.

• •• • • • •• • •• • ••• • • • •• •• ••• • ••• • •• • • • • •• • • • •• •• ••• • • •
• • •• •• • •

The historical, linguistic, genetic, and cultural evidence overwhelmingly supports the Uyghurs' status as the indigenous people of East Turkistan. Their deep-rooted heritage in the region, shaped by centuries of cultural exchange and adaptation, reflects an unbroken connection to their homeland.

The Uyghur identity is evident in the preservation of their language, traditions, and historical sites. Despite external influences, their cultural continuity underscores a long-standing presence that predates major political and demographic shifts in the region. The survival of Uyghur customs, literature, and religious practices further attests to their enduring bond with East Turkistan.

In summary, the Uyghurs are not recent migrants but an indigenous people whose history in East Turkistan spans thousands of years. Their contributions to the region's political and cultural landscape—ranging from their role in the Hun Empire, the ancient Tarim Basin Kingdoms, the Göktürks, and the Uyghur Khaganate to the development of the Qocho Kingdom and Karakhanid Khaganate—reinforce their deep-rooted presence.
East Turkistan's historical narrative reflects centuries of interaction and integration among various cultural groups, including the Tocharians, Saka, Huns, Ashina and Göktürks, and later the Uyghurs. Each of these groups played a significant role in shaping the region's identity, and their influences persist in the linguistic, genetic, and cultural heritage of modern Uyghurs.

Recognizing Uyghur indigeneity is essential to understanding their historical rights and cultural legacy in East Turkistan, which is deeply interwoven with the broader history of

Central Asian civilizations. Their story is one of resilience, continuity, and an enduring presence in their ancestral homeland.

Notes

72. *The Cambridge History of Early Inner Asia.* Edited by Denis Sinor. Cambridge: Cambridge University Press, 1990.
73. Golden, Peter B. *An Introduction to the History of the Turkic Peoples.* Wiesbaden: Otto Harrassowitz, 1992.
74. Hafiz-i Abru. *Zubdat al-Tawarikh.*
75. Sinor, Denis. "The Establishment and Role of the Turk Empire." In *The Cambridge History of Early Inner Asia*, edited by Denis Sinor, 285-314. Cambridge: Cambridge University Press, 1990.
76. Róna-Tas, András. *Hungarians and Europe in the Early Middle Ages: An Introduction to Early Hungarian History.* Budapest: Central European University Press, 1999.
77. Clauson, Gerard. *An Etymological Dictionary of Pre-Thirteenth-Century Turkish.* Oxford: Clarendon Press, 1972.
78. Taskin, V. S. *Materials on the History of the Ancient Turks.* Moscow: Nauka, 1984.
79. Findley, Carter Vaughn. *The Turks in World History.* Oxford: Oxford University Press, 2005.
80. Mair, Victor H., and J. P. Mallory. *The Tarim Mummies: Ancient China and the Mystery of the Earliest Peoples from the West.* London: Thames & Hudson, 2000.
81. Liu Mau-tsai. *Die Chinesischen Nachrichten zur Geschichte der Ost-Türken (T'u-Küe).* Wiesbaden: Harrassowitz, 1958.
82. Xu, Shuhua, et al. "Genetic Evidence for the Admixture of Eastern and Western Ancestry in Uyghurs." *American Journal of Human Genetics* 82, no. 4 (2008): 883-894.
83. Y-DNA Consortium. "Phylogenetic Relationships of Human Y-Chromosome Haplogroups." *Human Genetics* 127, no. 6 (2010): 651-658.
84. Di Cosmo, Nicola. *Ancient China and Its Enemies: The Rise of Nomadic Power in East Asian History.* Cambridge: Cambridge University Press, 2002.
85. Hansen, Valerie. *The Silk Road: A New History.* Oxford: Oxford University Press, 2012.
86. Beckwith, Christopher I. *Empires of the Silk Road: A History of Central Eurasia from the Bronze Age to the Present.* Princeton: Princeton University Press, 2009.
87. Kamalov, Ablet. "The Uyghurs as an Indigenous People of East Turkistan." *Central Asian Survey* 23, no. 3-4 (2004): 313-330.
88. Khojaev, Ablet. *The Uyghur Identity in Central Asia: Historical and Contemporary Perspectives.* Almaty: Central Asia Research Institute, 2018.

The *Oghuzname* is a cornerstone in the genesis and origin story of the Turkic peoples, including the Uyghurs. This foundational myth connects various Turkic tribes under a shared ancestor, Oghuz Khan, often referred to as the progenitor of all Turkic peoples. The *Turpan Oghuzname* and other sources frequently describe Oghuz Khan's people as Turks, symbolizing their unified identity under his leadership.^89 This narrative underscores his role in establishing the unity and prominence of the Turkic world.

The *Turpan Oghuzname*, an ancient Turkic epic, recounts his life and deeds. Discovered in the Turpan region of the Uyghur homeland, this version is believed to date back to the 9th to 12th centuries CE. Although its exact date remains uncertain, the text likely reflects pre-Islamic Turkic culture or the early Islamic period. Written in Old Turkic using the Uyghur script, it highlights the Uyghurs' role in preserving and shaping Turkic cultural narratives.^90

The narrative of Oghuz Khan blends history and mythology, emphasizing his role as a unifying figure for various Turkic tribes, including the Uyghurs. His story recounts his divine birth, rapid growth into a warrior, and conquests, symbolizing the expansion and dominance of the Turkic peoples.^92 Oghuz Khan's six sons—divided into two groups, the *Buzuks* (elder sons) and *Üchoks* (younger sons)—are credited with founding the various Turkic tribes. Each son ventured into new territories to conquer and settle, with their descendants forming the Turkic tribal names and identities, thereby linking their strength and unity to Oghuz Khan's lineage.

The *Oghuzname* details the origins of several Turkic tribes, weaving mythological narratives with historical undertones:

7.2.1 Karluk

The name Karluk derives from *qayarliq*, meaning "snow-covered." According to the *Oğuzname*, a Karluk noble retrieved Oghuz Khan's horse in snowy conditions, which led to the tribe's name. Historically, the Karluks were influential in the Tarim Basin and contributed significantly to modern Uyghur ancestry. Modern descendants of the Karluks include the Uzbeks, particularly in southern Uzbekistan and parts of Kyrgyzstan, and the Uyghurs.^93

7.2.2 Kangli

The Kangli people were named after the sound their wagons made during Oghuz Khan's campaigns, described as "kanga, kanga." This onomatopoeic origin reflects their role in transportation and logistics. Later, the Kangli became part of the Kipchak confederation.^94

7.2.3 Kipchak

A Kipchak noble helped Oghuz Khan cross a river by cutting down trees to form rafts. The sound of the rafts, "kanga, kanga," inspired their name. The Kipchaks became associated with practical solutions and adaptability. Modern Kipchak descendants include Kazakhs (especially those in the Middle Jüz), Kyrgyz, Crimean and Volga Tatars, Bashkirs, Nogais, and Turkic groups in the Caucasus such as the Karachays and Balkars.^95

7.2.4 Oghuz Tribes

The name Oghuz derives from Oghuz Khan, who is regarded as the eponymous ancestor of the Oghuz tribes. Historically, the Oghuz tribes played a transformative role in Central Asia, the Middle East, and beyond. Modern descendants of the Oghuz tribes include the Turks, particularly those descended from the Seljuks and Ottomans; Azerbaijanis, who share cultural and linguistic ties with the Turks; Turkmens, who are direct descendants of the Oghuz tribes in Central Asia; and the Gagauz, a predominantly Christian group in Moldova, Ukraine, and the Balkans.^96

• •• • • • • •• ••• ••• • •• ğ• • • • •

The Uyghurs play a prominent role in the *Oghuzname*, where Oghuz Khan declares himself "the Khagan of the Uyghurs" and extends his dominion to the "four corners of the world." This declaration underscores the Uyghurs' central role in the Turkic world and reflects their historical importance.^97

In another version of the *Oghuzname* from the 14th century, Rashid al-Din's *Jami' al-Tawarikh* mentions the Uyghurs among the tribes Oghuz Khan sought to unify. The term "Uyghur," associated with meanings like "united" or "allied," portrays the Uyghurs as obedient followers who readily accepted Oghuz Khan's leadership. This distinction highlights their loyalty and prominence within the Turkic confederation, contrasting them with other tribes that resisted his authority.^98

Oghuz Khan in *Oghuzname* : 'I am the Khagan of the Uyghur, who (thus) should be the Khagan of the four corners of the world.'

The *Turpan Oghuzname* codifies the Turkic origin story and underscores the Uyghurs' role in preserving and transmitting Turkic cultural traditions. By recording this foundational myth in Uyghur script, the Uyghurs ensured its survival through centuries of cultural shifts and Islamic influence. This manuscript highlights their intellectual and cultural leadership, emphasizing their pivotal role in shaping the Turkic world's historical and mythical narratives.^99

31

Notes

89. Peter B. Golden, *An Introduction to the History of the Turkic Peoples* (Wiesbaden: Harrassowitz Verlag, 1992), 190.
90. Denis Sinor, ed., *The Cambridge History of Early Inner Asia* (Cambridge: Cambridge University Press, 1990), 210.
91. Jonathan Ratcliffe, "Reappraising the Strata and Value of the Turpan Oğuz Nāme and Preliminary Translation," Monash University, 2022, 12.
92. Golden, *An Introduction to the History of the Turkic Peoples*, 195.
93. Golden, *An Introduction to the History of the Turkic Peoples*, 198.
94. Sinor, *The Cambridge History of Early Inner Asia*, 220.
95. Carter Vaughn Findley, *The Turks in World History* (New York: Oxford University Press, 2005), 87.
96. Golden, *An Introduction to the History of the Turkic Peoples*, 203.
97. Sinor, *The Cambridge History of Early Inner Asia*, 225.
98. Valerie Hansen, *The Silk Road: A New History with Documents* (New York: Oxford University Press, 2012), 112.
99. Ratcliffe, "Reappraising the Strata and Value of the Turpan Oğuz Nāme," 20.

From Empires to Exile: A Brief Uyghur History

The earliest references to the ancestors of the Uyghurs appear in Chinese historical records dating back to the 3rd to 4th centuries CE. These records describe their involvement as part of a larger group known as the Tiele (also called Toles). The Tiele were a confederation of nomadic tribes spread across the Central Asian steppes, occupying a region that extended from the Onon River in the east to the western steppes. Known for their distinctive high-wheeled wagons, the Tiele were adept herders and warriors, demonstrating remarkable mobility, determination and strength in the diverse and often harsh climates of Central Asia.^100

By the 1st century BCE, the Tiele were under the influence of the Xiongnu, often identified with the Huns. The Xiongnu formed a powerful nomadic empire controlling vast territories across the steppes. The Tiele, as part of this structure, contributed warriors and resources while adapting to the hierarchical framework established by the Xiongnu. However, internal conflicts and external pressures, including confrontations with Han China, weakened Xiongnu control, providing the Tiele with opportunities to assert their own identity.^101

During this period, the Tiele began to establish alliances with neighboring tribes and expand their influence within the steppe region. The collapse of Xiongnu dominance marked the first significant step in the rise of independent Tiele tribes, setting the stage for their increasing prominence in Central Asia. These developments also laid the groundwork for the emergence of Turkic tribal confederations in subsequent centuries.^102

In the 4th century CE, the Rouran Khanate emerged as the dominant power on the Central Asian steppes. This new khanate subjugated many of the Tiele tribes, including the ancestors of the Uyghurs. Under Rouran rule, the Tiele provided warriors and material

The Early Days: First Mention of the Uyghurs and the Tiele (Toles) Confederation

resources while maintaining their distinct identity. However, the Tiele tribes harbored growing resentment toward their Rouran overlords, which fostered a sense of unity and resistance among them.^103

Illustrations of the Tiele: Precursors of the Turkic Peoples, Including the Uyghurs

Despite their subjugation, the Tiele continued to evolve as a cohesive confederation. This period of domination and resistance was critical in shaping their political and social structures, enabling them to lay the foundation for future Turkic khanates. By the 6th century CE, the Tiele tribes would align with the emerging Göktürk Khaganate, overthrowing the Rouran and securing a prominent role in the political landscape of Central Asia.^104

• •• • • •• •• •• • • ••• • • • ••• • •• • ••• •• • • • • •••• • • ••••

The Tiele confederation was not a single unified entity but rather a loose alliance of tribes, each with its distinct leadership and cultural practices. Among these tribes were the ancestors of the Uyghurs, who began to emerge as a distinct group during the Tiele period. Historical accounts suggest that the Tiele were skilled in mounted warfare and renowned for their resilience, traits that became defining characteristics of the Turkic peoples, including the Uyghurs.^105

Chinese records such as the *Wei Shu* (Book of Wei) and *Sui Shu* (Book of Sui) document the Tiele's interactions with neighboring states and their contributions to regional politics. These sources emphasize the Tiele's strategic importance in the steppe region, describing

34

them as intermediaries between the northern steppes and the settled civilizations of East and Central Asia.^106

• •• • • • • • • •• •••• • •• •• •• ••• •• • • • • ••• •• •• ••

The legacy of the Tiele Confederation is deeply embedded in Uyghur history. As the Tiele transitioned into alliances with the Göktürk Khaganate and other Turkic empires, the foundations of Uyghur identity were solidified. The eventual rise of the Uyghur Khaganate in the 8th century CE was a direct continuation of the political and cultural developments initiated during the Tiele period. The Tiele's ability to maintain their identity through subjugation and alliance-building became a hallmark of Uyghur resilience, influencing their role as a dominant Turkic power in Central Asia.^107

Notes

100. Peter B. Golden, *An Introduction to the History of the Turkic Peoples* (Wiesbaden: Harrassowitz Verlag, 1992), 97–98.
101. Nicola Di Cosmo, *Ancient China and Its Enemies: The Rise of Nomadic Power in East Asian History* (Cambridge: Cambridge University Press, 2002), 120–122.
102. Golden, *An Introduction to the History of the Turkic Peoples*, 101.
103. Paul Buell, *The Avar Khaganate and the Western Turkic Khaganate* (Leiden: Brill, 2013), 54–56.
104. Golden, *An Introduction to the History of the Turkic Peoples*, 105.
105. Denis Sinor, ed., *The Cambridge History of Early Inner Asia* (Cambridge: Cambridge University Press, 1990), 121.
106. Ibid., 123.
107. Golden, *An Introduction to the History of the Turkic Peoples*, 108–109.

The Göktürk Khaganate

The Göktürk Khaganate, established in 552 AD, marked a transformative period for the Turkic peoples. As the first recorded Turkic empire, it unified various Turkic tribes under a single political entity, shaping the cultural and political landscape of Central Asia.

The Göktürks referred to themselves as *Türük Bodun* (𐰜𐰼𐰜:𐰉𐰆𐰑), meaning "Turkic Nation" or "Turkic People."[108] The term Göktürks or *Kök Türüks* (𐰚𐰇𐰜:𐱅𐰼𐰜), translating to "Celestial Turks," emphasized their divine connection to the heavens, a key element of their identity.[109]

The ruling Ashina clan unified numerous Turkic and allied tribes, including the Toquz Oğuz, Karluk, Basmil, and Türgiş. This unity underpinned the khaganate's strength and enduring influence across Central Asia.[110]

The Göktürk Khaganate originated in the regions of Altai Mountains under the leadership of Bumin Khagan, who led a rebellion against the Rouran Khaganate. Leveraging the Ashina clan's expertise in ironworking, Bumin rallied Turkic tribes and established the Göktürk Khaganate in 552 AD.[111]

Bumin's successor, Muhan Khagan, and his brother İstämi Khagan expanded the empire, securing control over the Mongolian steppes and extending influence to the Caspian Sea. Their dominance over Silk Road trade routes enhanced the empire's prosperity and political clout.[112]

At its zenith, the Göktürk Empire stretched from Manchuria to the Black Sea. Their control of Silk Road trade routes fostered cultural exchange and economic prosperity. The Göktürks collaborated with the Sogdians, whose expertise in trade and diplomacy bridged the empire with Eurasian markets. Taspar Khagan, a notable leader during this period, promoted Buddhism among Turkic elites while maintaining the traditional Tengrism faith.[113]

Following the death of Taspar Khagan, succession disputes fractured the empire. Civil wars in the 590s divided the Göktürks into Eastern and Western Khaganates, weakening their collective strength. The Tang Empire capitalized on these divisions, formalizing the split in 603 AD.^114

The Eastern Göktürks fell to Tang control in 630 AD, becoming vassals under Emperor Taizong. The Western Göktürks endured briefly but succumbed to internal strife and pressure from the Arab Caliphate by 659 AD, bringing Göktürk territories under Tang influence.^115

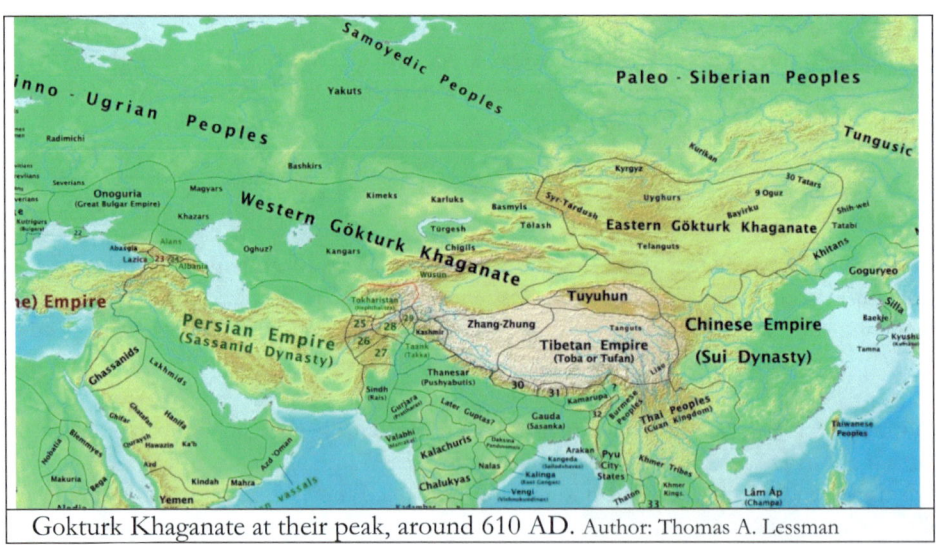
Gokturk Khaganate at their peak, around 610 AD. Author: Thomas A. Lessman

In 682 AD, Kutluk Khaghan, also known as Ilterish Khaghan, re-established the Göktürk state, laying the foundations of the Second Göktürk Khaganate. This revival came after years of turmoil following the collapse of the First Göktürk Khaganate, during which Turkic tribes had been subjugated by the Tang Empire. Kutluk's leadership, characterized by his military acumen and vision for unity, was instrumental in rallying fragmented Turkic tribes under his banner. With the support of his younger brother, Kapagan, a formidable military commander, and his trusted advisor, Tonyukuk, Kutluk not only restored the Göktürk state but also ushered in a period of political consolidation and cultural flourishing.

This resurgence is immortalized in the Orkhon Inscriptions, monumental carvings commissioned by Bilge Khagan, Kutluk's son, to commemorate the achievements of his father and uncle., reaffirming their sovereignty and identity in the Central Asian steppe.^116

This resurgence is immortalized in the Orkhon Inscriptions, monumental carvings commissioned by Bilge Khagan, Kutluk's son, to commemorate the achievements of his father and uncle., reaffirming their sovereignty and identity in the Central Asian steppe.^116

The Second Göktürk Khaganate fell in 744 AD, overtaken by the rising Uyghur tribes, marking the end of Göktürk dominance.

Göktürk society combined nomadic and semi-settled lifestyles, organized around clans led by *begs* (chiefs) under the khaghan's authority. Their spiritual beliefs centered on Tengrism, venerating Tengri, the god of the sky. Exposure to Buddhism, Zoroastrianism, and Christianity enriched their cultural fabric.^117

The Old Turkic script, exemplified by the Orkhon Inscriptions, stands as a testament to their literary and administrative sophistication. These inscriptions are among the earliest Turkic records, symbolizing unity and resilience.^118

The Göktürk Khaganate set the precedent for a unified Turkic state, influencing future empires such as the Uyghur Khaganate, the Seljuk Empire, and the Ottoman Empire. Their governance, cultural achievements, and impact on trade continue to resonate, cementing their place as progenitors of Turkic identity.^119

9.8.1 Toquz Oghuz(Nine Oghuz)

The Toquz Oghuzwere a confederation of nine tribes integral to the Göktürk Khaganate. They included key groups such as the Uyghurs, Basmils, and Bayırkus. Their alliance with the Ashina clan underpinned the empire's structure but also contributed to internal power struggles.^120

9.8.2 Karluk

The Karluks, referred to as the Uch Oghuzor "Three Oghuz," emerged as significant players during the late Göktürk period. Their eventual establishment of the Karakhanid Khaganate marked their transition to a dominant force in Central Asia.^121

9.8.3 Basmil

Initially vassals of the Göktürks, the Basmils briefly rose to prominence through alliances with the Tang Empire. Their ambitions, however, were curtailed by internal divisions and the growing influence of the Uyghurs and Karluks.^122

9.8.4 Türgiş

The Türgiş, an offshoot of the Western Göktürks, resisted Arab expansion into Central Asia. Despite their military efforts, internal disputes led to their subjugation by rival Turkic tribes.^123

9.8.5 Kyrgyz and Other Tribes

Other notable tribes included the Kyrgyz, who were located in the Yenisey region and renowned for their martial abilities, as well as Chik, Ediz, and Sir-Tardush contributed to the Göktürk Khaganate's diversity. Their shifting allegiances both strengthened and fractured the empire, highlighting the challenges of maintaining unity among diverse groups.^124

Notes

108. Peter B. Golden, *An Introduction to the History of the Turkic Peoples* (Wiesbaden: Harrassowitz Verlag, 1992), 97–98.
109. Denis Sinor, ed., *The Cambridge History of Early Inner Asia* (Cambridge: Cambridge University Press, 1990), 210.
110. Ibid., 214.
111. Nicola Di Cosmo, *Ancient China and Its Enemies* (Cambridge: Cambridge University Press, 2002), 120–122.
112. Golden, *An Introduction to the History of the Turkic Peoples*, 101.

113. Valerie Hansen, *The Silk Road: A New History with Documents* (Oxford: Oxford University Press, 2012), 88.
114. Sinor, *The Cambridge History of Early Inner Asia*, 220.
115. Hansen, *The Silk Road: A New History with Documents*, 91.
116. Golden, *An Introduction to the History of the Turkic Peoples*, 203.
117. Carter Vaughn Findley, *The Turks in World History* (New York: Oxford University Press, 2005), 87.
118. Hansen, *The Silk Road: A New History with Documents*, 92.
119. Golden, *An Introduction to the History of the Turkic Peoples*, 205.
120. Paul Buell, *The Avar Khaganate and the Western Turkic Khaganate* (Leiden: Brill, 2013), 54–56.
121. Golden, *An Introduction to the History of the Turkic Peoples*, 198.
122. Ibid., 201.
123. Sinor, *The Cambridge History of Early Inner Asia*, 223.
124. Buell, *Historical Dictionary of the Chinese World* (Lanham: Scarecrow Press, 2013), 117.

The Bilge Khagan and Köl Tegin Monuments, standing solemnly in Mongolia's Orkhon Valley, embodies the legacy of Bilge Khagan and his brother, the renowned general Köl Tegin. Together, they strove to preserve the Turkic identity, protect their people's sovereignty, and safeguard the wisdom of their ancestors. Erected in the 8th century, the monument's inscriptions in both Old Turkic and Chinese chronicle the experiences, trials, and hard-earned insights of the Turkic people, offering a timeless call to unity and resilience in the face of external threats. The deciphering of the inscriptions by Vilhelm Thomsen in 1893 marked a pivotal moment in Turkic studies, unveiling the linguistic and historical treasures of the Old Turkic script and solidifying the monument's importance in understanding Central Asian history.^125

Monument to Bilge Khagan, Orkhon valley, Mongolia

The Warning of Bilge Khagan and Köl Tegin: Unity and the Dangers of Foreign Influence

• • •• •• • • • • • ••• • • • •• • • • •

"People of Tokuz Oghuz, noble men! Hear my words with goodwill and listen attentively! To all groups—those in the east, the nearest on the south, those living to the west, and those furthest to the north—I address you with sincerity."^126

This address exemplifies the inclusive leadership of Bilge Khagan, calling for solidarity among the diverse Turkic tribes. His words reflect the shared responsibility of all Turkic peoples to maintain unity and safeguard their heritage.

• • •• • • ••• •••• • • • •• • ••• ••• • • • • •

The monument's inscriptions warn against the dangers of Chinese influence, which Bilge Khagan characterized as both alluring and destructive:

"The words of the Chinese are sweet, and their treasures—gold, silver, silk—are boundless. Through kindness and fine silk, they enchant even distant peoples, luring them close. But behind this charm lies deceit. With sweet words, they draw naive people to ruin, destroying families, tribes, and entire nations. Trusting in these charming words, the Turkic people nearly met their end."^127

The Chinese used enticing promises to lure the Turkic people away from their homeland:

"'If you are distant, you'll receive poor silk; if you come closer, we will give you the best.' Those who believed these words found death. The Turkic people were advised to settle in the Otuken Mountains, where they could live free and without sorrow, yet some were lured away to their detriment. In Otuken, the Turkic people would have maintained control over their destiny, united and secure."^128

This reflects the precarious balance between diplomacy and cultural survival, as Bilge Khagan sought to ensure the independence and unity of his people.

• • •• • • ••• •••• • ••• • •• • • • • •• ••• ••• • •• • •• •• • • ••

In a tone of wisdom gained through hardship, Bilge Khagan addressed his people directly:

"Once, the Turkic people were satisfied, free from hunger or hardship. But in our complacency, we ignored the wise words of our Khagan, wandered far and wide, and grew exhausted. Those who followed the deceptive calls faced great suffering. By the grace of God, I was chosen as Khagan and worked to change the

lives of the poor, who have since grown prosperous. Turkic noble men and people, I carved these words on stone so you will remember: united, we are strong; divided, we shall not survive."^129

This passage underscores the importance of unity and the lessons learned from past mistakes, reminding future generations of the consequences of division and complacency.

• • •• •• • • •• ••• •• • • ••• • •• ••• • •• • • •• • • • • ••• •

The inscriptions detail the devastating impact of Chinese influence on Turkic society:

"*Thus, the Chinese became impudent, acting with energy and deceit, turning relatives against each other and separating noble men from their people. The Turkic people dispersed, losing their supremacy, as the qayans who once unified the community were destroyed. Noble sons and beautiful daughters became slaves, and Turkic noble men, forgetting their own names, adopted Chinese ways and names.*"^130

This stark account highlights the erosion of Turkic identity, culture, and independence as a direct result of foreign manipulation.

• • •• • • •••••• •• • • •• •• •• • • • •• ••• • •

The monument's concluding message serves as a profound call to future generations, urging them to learn from the hardships and triumphs of their ancestors:

"*Let all Turkic people live.*"^131

This simple yet powerful statement encapsulates the essence of Bilge Khagan's warning: unity is the foundation of survival, and cultural integrity is the key to enduring independence. The inscriptions emphasize that the loss of unity and culture leads inevitably to the loss of sovereignty, humiliation, and destruction:

"*Without unity, our independence was lost. Those who succumbed to foreign influences abandoned their names and heritage, facing servitude and disgrace. Our noble sons and daughters became slaves, our traditions faded, and the proud Turkic spirit diminished. Let this be a warning: divided, we shall fall; united, we shall thrive.*"^132

The monument stands as a timeless reminder that cultural preservation and unity are inseparable from the survival and dignity of a people. It warns against the dangers of foreign allure and the devastating consequences of abandoning ancestral wisdom. Future generations are called to embrace their heritage, resist the seductive charm of external powers, and maintain solidarity to ensure their autonomy and prosperity.

Notes

125. Vilhelm Thomsen, Inscriptions de l'Orkhon Déchiffrées (Helsinki: Société Finno-Ougrienne, 1896).
126. Tekin, Talat. *A Grammar of Orkhon Turkic*. Bloomington: Indiana University, 1968, 10–18.
127. Ibid., 20.
128. Peter B. Golden, *An Introduction to the History of the Turkic Peoples* (Wiesbaden: Harrassowitz Verlag, 1992), 205; Denis Sinor, ed., *The Cambridge History of Early Inner Asia* (Cambridge: Cambridge University Press, 1990), 225.
129. Tekin, *A Grammar of Orkhon Turkic*, 30.
130. Golden, *An Introduction to the History of the Turkic Peoples*, 208; Tekin, *A Grammar of Orkhon Turkic*, 35
131. Tekin, Talat. *A Grammar of Orkhon Turkic*. Bloomington: Indiana University, 1968,38
132. Golden, Peter B. *An Introduction to the History of the Turkic Peoples*. Wiesbaden: Harrassowitz Verlag, 1992, 210; Tekin, *A Grammar of Orkhon Turkic*, 40.

The Uyghur Khaganate emerged as a successor to the Göktürks, as documented on the Bayanchur monument. Established in 744 AD, this powerful Turkic state extended its reach across Mongolia and Central Asia, wielding influence until 840 AD. Positioned strategically along the Silk Road, the Uyghur Khaganate reshaped Central Asian politics and left enduring cultural and diplomatic legacies, closely connected to the earlier Göktürk Empire.^133

• • •• • • • •• • • •

The official name of the Uyghur Khaganate was "Toquz Oγuz Budun" (𐰉𐰆𐰑𐰆𐰣:𐰉𐰆𐰑𐰆𐰣:𐰆𐰞𐰆𐰣), which translates to "Nine Tribes People." This term refers to the confederation of nine Turkic tribes, the Toquz Oghuz, forming the foundation of the Uyghur Khaganate. The name reflects the political structure and ethnic composition of the khaganate, as the Uyghurs initially belonged to the Toquz Oghuz alliance before rising to establish their own state in the 8th century.^134

• • •• • ••• •• • •• • • •• • ••• •• •• ••• ••

Following the fall of the Second Göktürk Khaganate, Kutlug Bilge Kül Khan founded the Uyghur Khaganate with support from the Karluks and Basmils. The capital, Ordu Balık (modern-day Karabalgasun, Mongolia), became the center of Uyghur power. The Toquz Oghuz were integral to the Uyghur Khaganate's military and political structure.^135

The two hypotheses examine the leadership and structure of the Toquz Oghuz, a confederation of nine tribes, in relation to the Uyghurs and the Yaglaqar clan. Haneda's hypothesis (1957) posits that the Toquz Oghuz were nine clans directly part of the Uyghur tribe, led by the Yaglaqar as their central leadership. In contrast, Golden's hypothesis (1992) argues that the Toquz Oghuz were a broader coalition of nine tribes, distinct from but led by the Uyghurs, who themselves consisted of nine subtribes managed by the

Yaglaqar. Supporting this, the Shine Usu inscription reveals that the Yaglaqar ruled over both the "Ten Tribes Uyghur" and the "Nine Tribes Oghuz," highlighting a layered political and tribal hierarchy.^136

• • •• •• •• • • •• • • • • • • •• • •• •••• • ••• • • • • • ••• • • • • • • • ••

The early expansion of the Uyghur Khaganate was marked by its rapid consolidation of power and the subjugation of rival Turkic tribes. Following the fall of the Second Göktürk Khaganate in 744 AD, the Uyghurs, led by Kutlug Bilge Kül Khan, quickly established dominance over former Göktürk territories in Mongolia. Through military campaigns and strategic alliances, the Khaganate absorbed key Turkic groups such as the Karluks, Türgish, and Kirghiz, transforming the Uyghurs into the leading Turkic power in Central Asia.^137

By the reign of Bayanchur Khan (747–759 AD), the Uyghurs had solidified control across Mongolia, eastern regions of the East Turkistan, and parts of southern Siberia. Bayanchur Khan expanded Uyghur influence particularly in the Turpan Basin and Kucha, securing critical sections of the Silk Road and exerting indirect influence over Zhetysu (modern southeastern Kazakhstan) through alliances with Turkic tribes.^138 However, rivalry with the Tibetan Empire persisted in the Tarim Basin, where control of cities like Kashgar and Khotan often shifted.^139

The Tang Empire indirectly controlled the Tarim Basin during its peak (640s–8th century CE) by relying on local Turkic rulers to manage the region. A key figure was Ashina She'er (r. 655–679 AD), a Turkic general of the Ashina clan, who governed on behalf of the Tang after the collapse of the Western Türk Khaganate. Ashina She'er played a crucial role in solidifying Tang authority in the Tarim Basin by commanding local Turkic tribes and ensuring their loyalty to the Tang.^140

The Battle of Talas in 751 AD marked a turning point in Central Asian geopolitics. Tang forces under Gao Xianzhi, supported by Karluk allies, faced the Abbasid Caliphate but suffered a decisive defeat when the Karluks switched allegiance to the Abbasids. This event curtailed Tang expansion into Central Asia, including modern East Turkistan, and highlighted the shifting allegiances among Turkic tribes.^141

• • •• • • ••• •• • ••• •• • •• • • ••• • ••• • •• ••• • • •• • • • ••

Bögü Khan (759–779), the son of Bayanchur Khan, ruled during a transformative period for the Uyghur Khaganate. In 763 AD, while aiding the Tang Empire during the An Lushan Rebellion, Bögü Khan encountered Manichaean priests whose teachings captivated him. Inspired, he returned to his capital, Ordu Balık, and adopted Manichaeism as the state religion.^142 This marked a cultural and religious transition for the Uyghurs, as they moved away from their traditional Turkic beliefs and embraced a settled lifestyle centered on trade, spirituality, and religious study.^143

Manichaeism's emphasis on asceticism and peace spurred the construction of Manichaean temples across Uyghur-controlled territory. The Uyghurs adopted a script based on the Sogdian alphabet, which became crucial for religious and administrative functions, facilitating the recording and dissemination of Manichaean texts. This religious shift encouraged urban development, transforming Ordu Balık, Turpan, and other cities in the Tarim Basin into hubs of trade, cultural exchange, and religious diversity along the Silk Road.^144

• • •• • • •••••• ••• • • •• • ••• •• •••• • • • • • • • •• •• •••• • •• • • • •• •• • •••

The Uyghur Khaganate was widely acknowledged as the de facto leader of the Turkic world during their reign. Their political and spiritual authority positioned them as the rightful successors to the Göktürks, symbolizing a unifying force among Turkic tribes.^145 Their influence extended across vast regions, encompassing modern-day Mongolia, East Turkistan, Kyrgyzstan, and Kazakhstan, largely supported by strategic alliances and military campaigns.^145

The Uyghur Khagans demonstrated exceptional leadership, setting standards for governance, diplomacy, and cultural development that were emulated by other Turkic groups. Their ability to mediate between Turkic tribes and neighboring powers, including the Tang Empire, showcased their diplomatic expertise and elevated their political stature. By skillfully governing both urban centers and nomadic territories, they reinforced their status as adaptable and unifying leaders in the Turkic world. This legacy of governance and cultural influence persisted long after the fall of their Khaganate in 840.^146

• • •• • • • • • • •• • • • • • • ••• •• • • • • •• • • • • • • ••• • •• ••• • •

Under Bögü Khan, the Uyghurs commanded Silk Road trade routes, ushering in economic prosperity. Uyghur merchants, escorted by military guards, exchanged silk, tea, and luxury goods. The Tang Empire sought alliances with the Uyghurs, establishing marriage ties and bestowing tributes of silk to maintain Uyghur support.^147 Sogdian influences also enriched Uyghur society, as they adopted elements of Sogdian art, literature, and culture, transforming the Uyghur Khaganate into a multicultural empire known for its cosmopolitanism.^147

Despite cultural and economic achievements, the Uyghur Khaganate's adoption of Manichaeism led to a decrease in martial skills among its warriors, making it vulnerable to external threats. In 840 AD, internal conflict and the invasion by the Kirghiz led to the fall of the Uyghur Khaganate. With a force of around 80,000 horsemen, the Kirghiz defeated the Uyghurs, capturing Ordu Balık and killing the khagan Kurebir. In 846, the last Uyghur khagan, Öge, was killed after having spent his 6-year reign fighting the Kirghiz and Tang Empire. This marked the end of Uyghur rule in Mongolia.^148

After the fall, many Uyghurs migrated south to the Tarim Basin, establishing the Qocho Uyghur Kingdom, which continued as a center of Buddhist learning. Another group settled in the Hexi Corridor near Ganzhou, forming a smaller Uyghur state that lasted until the Tangut conquest in 1036. After the fall of the Uyghur state in Ganzhou, some Uyghurs remained in the vicinity of Ganzhou, while others migrated to the Etsin-kol region in the Gobi Desert. A portion of these Uyghurs continued their westward movement and eventually joined the Cumans and Kipchaks on the Pontic-Caspian Steppe.^149 The Karluks migrated westward to the Tengri Tagh and Syr Darya regions, eventually founding the Kara-Khanid Khanate, while the Shatuo Turks moved into Tang China and rose to prominence during the Five Dynasties period. Meanwhile, the Kirghiz occupied the former Uyghur territories in Mongolia, but their dominance was short-lived, leaving the region fragmented. These migrations not only established new states but also facilitated cultural, religious, and economic transformations across Central Asia.^150

The Uyghur Khaganate left a lasting legacy in Central Asia, with the Qocho Uyghur Kingdom bridging the Turkic and Chinese worlds and fostering cultural exchange. The Uyghurs' development of scripts and transmission of Buddhist and Manichaean texts enriched Central Asia's intellectual landscape, making their cities hubs of art, literature, and trade.^151

From Empires to Exile: A Brief Uyghur History

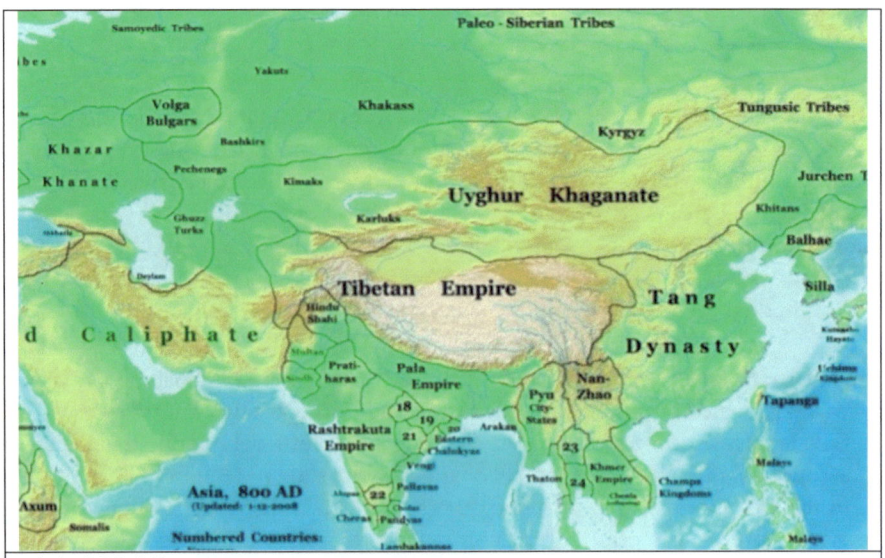

Asia 800 AD. Author: Thomas A. Lessman. Source URL: http://www.ThomasLessman.com/History/images/East-Hem_800ad.jpg.

A mural of an Uyghur Khagan, dated around 8th century.	Uyghur Soldiers from QaraShahr. Source: Le, Le, Coq Albert von. "Von Land und Leuten in Ostturkistan Berichte und Abenteuer der 4. deutschen Turfanexpedition. 1926

From Confederation to Empire: The Uyghur Khaganate's Journey Through Central Asia

Bayanchur Khagan (also known as Mo-yen-cho in Chinese sources) was a prominent ruler of the Uyghur Khaganate, reigning from 747 to 759. His inscriptions, found on the Şine-Usu (Shine Us) monument in Mongolia, offer unique insight into his reflections on his rule, his lineage, and his ancestors. The inscription is written in Old Turkic using the Orkhon script, similar to the inscriptions of the Göktürks. A translation from the Şine-Usu inscription, dedicated by Bayanchur Khan to his achievements and heritage, reads:

"I am Bayanchur, the wise Khagan, blessed by the Heavens, who was appointed to rule. I became the ruler of the Turkic nation; I became the sovereign over the Turks. My father ruled and organized the nation. He granted honor and titles to the noblemen of the land. With my noble lords and my people, I led the Turks forward. With the wisdom and teachings of my father, I united the realm and preserved the lineage. My father, a wise and powerful ruler, took hold of the state, took care of the people, and established order. The Turkic people, together with my lords and nobility, should not be left to perish. With the grace of the Heavens and through my rule, I safeguarded the state and the people"[152]

Bayanchur Khagan's inscriptions at the Şine-Usu monument reference his Turkic ancestors and their achievements, establishing a direct link to the legacy of the Göktürk Khagans. He explicitly acknowledges the contributions of Bumın Khagan and İstemi Khagan, the founding figures of the Göktürk Khaganate, thus grounding the Uyghur Khaganate's authority in the lineage of these illustrious leaders. This connection serves to reinforce the continuity and legitimacy of the Uyghur Khaganate by linking it to the prestigious lineage of the Göktürks:

"My ancestors, Bumın Khagan and İstemi Khagan, held the state and maintained the order. Both were illustrious rulers, leading tens of thousands of people. For the sake of the Turkic people, they governed the nation and upheld the traditions. They were strong leaders for a powerful nation. Let the Turkic people not perish, let the nation not fall apart!"[153]

These inscriptions underscore Bayanchur Khan's aim to position the Uyghur Khaganate within the esteemed lineage of the Göktürks, reinforcing the continuity of Turkic governance and cultural unity, with a focus on the preservation and protection of the Turkic people under the divine mandate of Heaven.

Notes

133. Denis Sinor, ed., *The Cambridge History of Early Inner Asia* (Cambridge: Cambridge University Press, 1990).
134. Peter B. Golden, *An Introduction to the History of the Turkic Peoples* (Wiesbaden: Otto Harrassowitz, 1992).
135. Yuri Bregel, *An Historical Atlas of Central Asia* (Leiden: Brill, 2003).

136. History Studies, Haneda Tōru, "Old Book of Tang" and "New Book of Tang," translated by Golden, 1992.
137. Denis Sinor, ed., *The Cambridge History of Early Inner Asia* (Cambridge: Cambridge University Press, 1990).
138. Peter B. Golden, *An Introduction to the History of the Turkic Peoples* (Wiesbaden: Otto Harrassowitz, 1992).
139. James Millward, *Eurasian Crossroads: A History of Xinjiang* (New York: Columbia University Press, 2007).
140. Denis Sinor, ed., *The Cambridge History of Early Inner Asia* (Cambridge: Cambridge University Press, 1990).
141. James Millward, *Eurasian Crossroads: A History of Xinjiang* (New York: Columbia University Press, 2007).
142. Colin Mackerras, "The Uighur Empire According to the T'ang Dynastic Histories: A Study in Sino-Uighur Relations 744-840," *Central Asiatic Journal* 16, no. 3 (1972): 207–241.
143. Peter B. Golden, *An Introduction to the History of the Turkic Peoples* (Wiesbaden: Otto Harrassowitz, 1992).
144. James Millward, *Eurasian Crossroads: A History of Xinjiang* (New York: Columbia University Press, 2007).
145. Peter B. Golden, *An Introduction to the History of the Turkic Peoples* (Wiesbaden: Otto Harrassowitz, 1992).
146. Denis Sinor, ed., *The Cambridge History of Early Inner Asia* (Cambridge: Cambridge University Press, 1990).
147. James Millward, *Eurasian Crossroads: A History of Xinjiang* (New York: Columbia University Press, 2007).
148. John W. Dardess, *Governing China: 150–1850* (Hackett Publishing, 2010).
149. Peter B. Golden, *An Introduction to the History of the Turkic Peoples* (Wiesbaden: Otto Harrassowitz, 1992).
150. Denis Sinor, ed., *The Cambridge History of Early Inner Asia* (Cambridge: Cambridge University Press, 1990).
151. Yuri Bregel, *An Historical Atlas of Central Asia* (Leiden: Brill, 2003).
152. Tekin, Talat. *A Grammar of Orkhon Turkic.* Bloomington: Indiana University, 1968.
153. Sergei G. Klyashtorny and V. Livshits, *The Tariat Inscriptions and the History of the Uyghur Empire.* Moscow: Nauka, 1972.

The Uyghurs were part of the Toquz Oghuz, a powerful confederation of nine Turkic clans in the early medieval period. The Toquz Oghuz were prominent during the Göktürk Khaganate as part of the Tiele tribal union, and they rose to central importance under the leadership of the Uyghurs, who established the Uyghur Khaganate in 744 AD. The Uyghur Khaganate identified itself as the Toquz Oghuz Budun, reflecting its foundational ties to this tribal confederation. This name underscores the Uyghurs' role as a central element of the Toquz Oghuz and highlights their historical significance in shaping the broader Turkic world.^152

Peter B. Golden, a renowned scholar of Turkic and Central Asian history, extensively analyzed the political, social, and cultural dynamics of early Turkic peoples, including the Oğuz, and provided valuable insights into the historical role of the Toquz Oğuz. Modern national and regional histories often emphasize the Oghuz's role in Islamic and Middle Eastern history, particularly through the Seljuks and Ottomans, or their contributions to Turkic identity in Central Asia and Anatolia, overshadowing the Toquz Oghuz, who were more connected to the Uyghur-led polity of the eastern steppe. Scholars like Peter Golden highlight the need to explore the interconnectedness between these early confederations, recognizing their dynamic and fluid identities that contributed foundationally, albeit indirectly, to the later Oghuz trajectory and achievements.^153

According to Golden, the term "Oghuz" originally referred to a tribal union or kinship group, and the Toquz Oghuz represented a specific tribal organization within the broader framework of Turkic alliances. The confederation emerged as a distinct group in the 7th century during the Second Türk Khaganate. The Toquz Oghuz were significant players during the Second Türk Khaganate and later under the Uyghur Khaganate. They were often both allies and rivals of the ruling Türk and Uyghur Khagans. This dual role is documented in various inscriptions, such as those of Bilge Khagan and Kül Tigin, where the Toquz Oghuz are described as both "my own people" and "rebellious subjects."^154 Their strategic position and military strength made them key factors in the stability or instability of these empires. Rebellions by the Toquz Oghuz against central authority often contributed to the downfall of the Türk Khaganate and, later, the Uyghur Khaganate.^155

The mid-8th-century Tariat inscriptions, dedicated to Uyghur Khagan Bayanchur, reference the rebellious Igdir tribe as "my people," which had revolted against him. Mahmud al-Kashgari later lists the Igdir as the 14th of the 22 Oghuz tribes, further supporting the longstanding connections among these groups.^156 Historian S. G. Klyashtorny views this as "direct evidence in favor of the existence of kindred relations between the Toquz Oghuzs of Mongolia, the Guzs of the Aral region, and modern Turkmens."^157 While there are connections between the Toquz Oghuz and later Oghuz tribes, the evolution of these groups into entities like the Oghuz Yabghu State in Western Turkistan reflects a shared origin and complex tribal realignments rather than a direct, linear development.^158

Golden argues that the fall of the Uyghur Khaganate in 840 AD was a turning point for the Oghuz tribes. In the following decades, groups of Oghuz tribes began migrating westward across Central Asia. This was not a single, unified migration but a series of movements spurred by factors like the collapse of the Uyghur state, pressure from other nomadic tribes such as the Kirghiz, and the lure of fertile lands along the Syr Darya and rich pastures near the Aral Sea. By the 9th century, the Oghuz had established themselves in Western Turkistan, encountering new political realities. Islamic geographers and historians began to notice this powerful confederation on their borders. The Oghuz were described as a formidable force influencing the regional balance of power—raiders, traders, and at times, mercenaries for Islamic rulers.^159 However, claims of a migration during Caliph al-Mahdi's reign (775–785 CE) remain speculative, as evidence of Oghuz interactions with the Islamic world becomes more prominent only in later centuries.^160

Ibn al-Athir, a 13th-century Islamic scholar, mentioned the Oghuz in his chronicles, noting their interactions with Islamic states during the reign of the Abbasid Caliphs. This migration and settlement laid the foundation for the later Seljuk Empire, which traced its origins to the Oghuz tribes.^161 This migration and integration into Islamic societies gave rise to powerful empires like the Seljuk and Ottoman dynasties, where Oghuz heritage remained significant. Their legacy endures through cultural traditions, Turkic languages, and historical narratives, notably contributing to the Turkic-Islamic synthesis that shaped much of Central Asia and the Middle East.^162

Notes

152.   Peter B. Golden, *An Introduction to the History of the Turkic Peoples* (Wiesbaden: Otto Harrassowitz, 1992), 145-147.

153. Ibid., 145-147.
154. Tekin, Talat. *Orkhon Inscriptions*. Bloomington: Indiana University, 1968, 261-263.
155. Denis Sinor, ed., *The Cambridge History of Early Inner Asia* (Cambridge: Cambridge University Press, 1990), 285-286.
156. Mahmud al-Kashgari, *Diwan Lughat al-Turk*, trans. Robert Dankoff (Cambridge: Harvard University Press, 1982).
157. Sergei G. Klyashtorny, *Turkic Inscriptions of the Tariat Valley* (Moscow: Nauka, 1972).
158. Peter B. Golden, *An Introduction to the History of the Turkic Peoples* (Wiesbaden: Otto Harrassowitz, 1992), 149-150.
159. Ibid., 151-153.
160. V. V. Barthold, *Turkestan Down to the Mongol Invasion* (London: Luzac & Co., 1968), 351-352.
161. Ibn al-Athir, *The Chronicle of Ibn al-Athir for the Crusading Period from al-Kamil fi'l-Ta'rikh*, trans. D. S. Richards (Aldershot: Ashgate, 2006), Vol. 1, 75-76.
162. Clifford E. Bosworth, *The Ghaznavids: Their Empire in Afghanistan and Eastern Iran 994–1040* (Edinburgh: Edinburgh University Press, 1968), 10-12.

The term "Karakhanid" is a modern label; contemporary titles emphasized their Turkic roots and authority. Historian Ibn al-Athir called them el-Hâniyyetü'l-Etrâk ("Khans of the Turks") to highlight their strong Turkic identity.^163 Historians like al-Tabari, Makdisi, and Juzjani referred to them as Al-i Afrasiyab ("House of Afrâsiyâb"), linking them to the legendary figure Afrâsiyâb.^164 Mahmud al-Kashgari described them as Khâqânî ("Khaganate"), underscoring their supreme status among the Turks.^165 Turkish historian Ömer Soner Hunkan used Türk Hakanlığı ("Turkic Khaganate") to reflect their role within Turkic society.^166

Following the 840 CE collapse of the Uyghur Khaganate, the Karluks consolidated power in Central Asia, leveraging alliances and military strength.^167 Historians like Ibn al-Athir and al-Mas'udi noted the Karluks' Ashina clan connections, further legitimizing their power.^168 Their conversion to Islam transformed the political landscape, establishing the Karakhanids as the first Muslim Turkic empire in Central Asia.

The Karakhanid Khaganate consisted of Karluk and allied Turkic tribes, primarily the Karluks, Yaghma, and Chigil. The Karluks initially settled in the Tengri Tagh and Chu Valley, playing a key role in forming the Karakhanid state. The Yaghma, another Toquz Oghuz-origin tribe, resided near the Tarim Basin and Kashgar, while the Chigil inhabited the Issyk-Kul region and the Ferghana Valley.^169 Around 746 CE, the Karluks emerged as an independent force after revolting against the Türgesh Khaganate, later asserting control over the central Tengri Tagh region. Their alliance with the Abbasid Caliphate in the 751 CE Battle of Talas strengthened their position and curtailed Chinese expansion in Central Asia, consolidating Karluk control over Silk Road trade routes.^170

The Karakhanid Khaganate

In the late 10th century, the Karakhanids expanded significantly, solidifying their influence in Central Asia. Their first major conquest was Kashgar, a key administrative and cultural center, followed by control over the Tarim Basin, including Yarkent and Khotan.^171 The Karakhanids reached their peak in 999 by capturing Bukhara and Samarkand, marking the end of the Samanid dynasty and establishing the Karakhanids as the dominant power in Transoxiana, covering much of modern Uzbekistan. Their empire also encompassed cities like Tashkent (modern Uzbekistan), Taraz (Kazakhstan), Osh (Kyrgyzstan), and parts of the Ferghana Valley.^172

To manage their vast territories, the Karakhanid realm divided around 1040 into two branches: the Western Karakhanids governed from Samarkand and Bukhara, while the Eastern Karakhanids ruled from Kashgar and Balasagun.^173

Word Map in 1000 AD. Author: Thomas A. Lessman. Source URL: https://commons.wikimedia.org/wiki/File:Ghaznavid_map_1000_ad.jpg

56

The Karakhanids played a central role in blending Islamic scholarship with Turkic traditions, establishing madrasas and mosques in cities like Bukhara, Samarkand, and Kashgar. This foundation enriched the Silk Road not only as a trade route but as a pathway for intellectual exchange.^174 They built upon the scholarly legacy of the Qocho Uyghur Kingdom, shifting from Buddhist to Islamic influences and establishing Turkic as a written language within an Islamic state.^175

Their contributions laid the groundwork for subsequent Turkic-Islamic civilizations, including the Khwarazmian Empire and later the Timurid Empire, both of which advanced Turkic-Islamic scholarship. The Chagatai Khanate and Yarkent Khanate continued the Karakhanid legacy, fostering Turkic-Islamic culture in the Tarim Basin and beyond, emphasizing Turkic identity within an Islamic context.^176

The Karakhanids maintained relationships with the Seljuk Empire, the Ghaznavids, and the Kara-Khitai. In the 11th century, the Seljuks exerted military pressure on the Karakhanids, leading to a period of decline and vassalage for the Western branch.^177 In the east, the Kara-Khitai subjugated the Eastern Karakhanids in the mid-12th century, reducing their autonomy, though the khaganate continued nominal rule until the early 13th century.^178

Internal fragmentation, succession disputes, and external pressures accelerated the Karakhanids' decline. The Western Karakhanids, weakened by conflicts with the Seljuks and later the Khwarazmian Empire, gradually lost influence. The Eastern Karakhanids, under Kara-Khitai subjugation, struggled to control their remaining territories. By 1211, the Khwarazmian Empire conquered the Western Karakhanid state, and in 1218, the Mongol Empire absorbed the Eastern territories, marking the khaganate's end.^179

The Karakhanids left a profound legacy, instrumental in Islamizing the region and integrating Islamic values with Turkic traditions. Their support for scholarship influenced later Turkic dynasties, including the Khwarazmian, Chagatai, and Timurid empires, shaping Central Asia's historical and cultural trajectory.^180 Their realm spanned modern Uzbekistan, Kazakhstan, Kyrgyzstan, Tajikistan, and East Turkistan, uniting diverse territories under a single Islamic state and leaving an indelible mark on the region.^181

Notes

163. Ibn al-Athir, *The Complete History*.
164. Al-Tabari, Makdisi, and Juzjani, *House of Afrâsiyâb*.
165. Mahmud al-Kashgari, *Diwan Lughat al-Turk*, trans. Robert Dankoff (Cambridge: Harvard University Press, 1982).
166. Ömer Soner Hunkan, *Türk Hakanlığı – Karahanlılar* (Istanbul: Ötüken, 2015).
167. Michal Biran, *The Empire of the Karakhanids* (Leiden: Brill, 2005), 47-49.
168. Ibn al-Athir, *The Complete History*; al-Mas'udi, *The Meadows of Gold*.
169. Peter B. Golden, *An Introduction to the History of the Turkic Peoples* (Wiesbaden: Otto Harrassowitz, 1992), 236-238.
170. Denis Sinor, ed., *The Cambridge History of Early Inner Asia* (Cambridge: Cambridge University Press, 1990), 304-306.
171. Michal Biran, *The Empire of the Karakhanids* (Leiden: Brill, 2005), 67-69.
172. Peter B. Golden, *An Introduction to the History of the Turkic Peoples* (Wiesbaden: Otto Harrassowitz, 1992), 239-241.
173. Denis Sinor, ed., *The Cambridge History of Early Inner Asia* (Cambridge: Cambridge University Press, 1990), 308-310.
174. Michal Biran, *The Empire of the Karakhanids* (Leiden: Brill, 2005), 70-73.
175. Peter B. Golden, *An Introduction to the History of the Turkic Peoples* (Wiesbaden: Otto Harrassowitz, 1992), 250-252.
176. Michal Biran, *The Empire of the Karakhanids* (Leiden: Brill, 2005), 79-81.
177. Denis Sinor, ed., *The Cambridge History of Early Inner Asia* (Cambridge: Cambridge University Press, 1990), 308-310.
178. Michal Biran, *The Empire of the Karakhanids* (Leiden: Brill, 2005), 79-81.
179. Peter B. Golden, *An Introduction to the History of the Turkic Peoples* (Wiesbaden: Otto Harrassowitz, 1992), 242-244.
180. Ibid., 246-248.
181. Michal Biran, *The Empire of the Karakhanids* (Leiden: Brill, 2005), 79-81; Denis Sinor, ed., *The Cambridge History of Early Inner Asia* (Cambridge: Cambridge University Press, 1990), 308-310.

S ultan Satuq Bughrakhan (895–956) is celebrated as a legendary figure, known for his profound faith, visionary leadership, and role in establishing the Karakhanid state as the first Muslim Turkic empire. Following the death of his father, the young prince and heir to the Karakhanid throne was raised under the guardianship of his uncle, Oghulchak Khan, a staunch proponent of Buddhism and Manichaeism. However, Satuq's destiny took an extraordinary turn in the culturally dynamic city of Kashgar, where he encountered the teachings of Islam through the influence of a Persian Samanid missionary, Abu Nasr, setting the stage for a transformative journey.[182]

Growing up in a bustling Silk Road center where various religions and ideas converged, Satuq developed a fascination with Islam. Abu Nasr, a devout missionary who had taken refuge in Kashgar, built a mosque in Artush to serve the Muslim merchants and travelers, with the blessing of Oghulchak, who allowed him to practice Islam but forbade proselytizing. Satuq's clandestine visits to the mosque ignited a passion within him, and the guidance of Abu Nasr, along with the devotion he observed among Muslim merchants, eventually led him to embrace Islam. At the age of 12, he formally converted, adopting the name "Abd al-Karim"—a new identity that foreshadowed his future as a unifier under Islam.[183]

One of the most famous quotes attributed to Satuq, recorded in the *Tazkira-i Bughrakhan*, reflects the determination that would define his mission:

"If God has chosen me to be His servant and to carry His word to my people, then I shall do so with all my strength, even if it means confronting my own kin. For in faith, there is no division between brothers and enemies. All are equal in the sight of the Almighty."[184]

Emboldened by his faith, Satuq quietly gathered followers among fellow converts and Muslim merchants in Kashgar and Artush. He later openly defied his uncle Oghulchak, rallying support for a rebellion against non-Islamic rule. With aid from the Samanids, Satuq successfully conquered Kashgar, declaring it the first Muslim capital of the Karakhanid state. In 942, he advanced toward Balasagun, where he ultimately defeated his uncle in a decisive battle, establishing a unified Muslim state. His conquests continued, with cities such as Talas, Samarkand, Osh, and Shash falling under his rule, symbolizing a united Turkic identity grounded in Islam.^186

Satuq's conversion set off a transformative wave among the Turkic tribes. Muslim historians, including Ibn Miskawaih and Ibn al-Athir, recount that following his conversion, there was a massive shift toward Islam among the Turkic nomads. According to these accounts, approximately 200,000 tents—representing an extensive community of Turkic families—converted to Islam, influenced by Satuq's faith and leadership. This large-scale conversion symbolized a significant shift in Central Asian history, establishing Islam as a unifying force for the Turkic tribes.^185

Satuq's reign extended beyond military victories. Deeply committed to justice, equality, and intellectual growth, he laid the groundwork for a vibrant Islamic society. He initiated the construction of mosques and madrasas, encouraging Islamic scholarship and cultural development across his territories. He also abolished slavery, demonstrating his commitment to equality. The intellectual legacy he fostered continued through his descendants, inspiring the emergence of renowned scholars like Yusuf Has Hajib and Mahmud Kashgari, who enriched the Turkic-Islamic heritage Satuq had helped to shape.^187

Satuq's leadership was marked by visionary policies that ensured prosperity and stability. He established an annual council known as the "Tertiary Panel," where state matters were discussed, demonstrating his commitment to structured governance. Satuq also encouraged economic growth by reducing trade taxes and supporting agriculture, which bolstered the region's economy. His military strategies included reinforcing borders and fortifying defenses, safeguarding his kingdom from external threats and ensuring the continued spread of Islam throughout the Turkic lands.^188

Satuq Bughra Khan ruled for four decades, transforming the Karakhanid Khanate into a thriving Islamic state. Near the end of his life, he expressed his wish to be buried close to his mentor, Abu Nasr, in Artush near Kashgar. His mausoleum, constructed after his death in 956, became a revered muslim site, honoring his legacy as a spiritual and political leader. His life and achievements are immortalized in works like the *Tazkira-i Bughrakhan*, a historical and hagiographical biography, and in Seypudin Aziz's novel *Satuk Bugra Khan*, both of which celebrate him as a saintly figure and a formidable ruler.^189

Sultan Satuq Bughrakhan remains an enduring symbol of resilience, leadership, and faith as the first Muslim ruler in the Turkic world. His unifying vision brought diverse Turkic tribes together under a shared Islamic faith, establishing a legacy that would shape Central Asian history for centuries. His mausoleum near Kashgar stands as a testament to his influence, drawing visitors and scholars who seek to understand the depth of his impact on Turkic and Islamic civilization. His legacy continued through his descendants, who strengthened the Turkic-Islamic identity that endures to this day.^190

Prince Satuq met Abu Nasr, an Islamic missionary in Artush, marking his pivotal conversion to Islam and the beginning of a transformative era in Central Asian history.	The tomb of Satuq Bughra Khan, situated within a mosque in Artush, near the historic city of Kashgar

Notes

182. *Tazkira-i Bughrakhan*; Hudud al-'Alam.
183. Sallahiat Mullah Haji, *Tazkira-i Bughrakhan*.
184. Ibid.
185. Ibn Miskawaih, *The Experiences of the Nations*; Ibn al-Athir, *The Complete History*.
186. Peter B. Golden, *An Introduction to the History of the Turkic Peoples* (Wiesbaden: Otto Harrassowitz, 1992), 214-216.
187. Michal Biran, *The Empire of the Karakhanids* (Leiden: Brill, 2005), 70-73.
188. Ibid.
189. Sallahiat Mullah Haji, *Tazkira-i Bughrakhan*.
190. Peter B. Golden, *An Introduction to the History of the Turkic Peoples* (Wiesbaden: Otto Harrassowitz, 1992), 246-248.

From Empires to Exile: A Brief Uyghur History

Yusuf Qadir Khan rose to prominence within the Karakhanid Khaganate, ascending to the throne in 1024 (415 AH) after his predecessor, Mansur, abdicated to pursue a life of spiritual devotion. Before his ascension, Yusuf had already established his reputation as an effective and strategic leader, serving as governor of Khotan and later Bukhara. These roles reinforced his status within the Karakhanid realm and laid a foundation for his authority and capabilities as ruler.^191

In 1006, Yusuf led a successful campaign against the Kingdom of Khotan, a significant Buddhist center in the Tarim Basin. This victory ended Buddhist rule in Khotan, establishing Islam as the region's primary faith and marking a pivotal moment in the Karakhanid expansion. Yusuf subsequently directed expeditions toward the Uyghur Kingdom of Qocho near Turpan. Although he did not fully subjugate Qocho during his reign, these campaigns weakened the Uyghur state, ultimately paving the way for its integration into the Turkic-Islamic sphere of influence.^192

Beyond eastern conquests, Yusuf safeguarded the Karakhanid state from external threats, notably from the Ghaznavids and Seljuqs. Though temporarily displaced from some territories by Mahmud of Ghazni, Yusuf managed to reclaim his lands, reinforcing strategic cities like Samarkand and Bukhara. These cities later flourished as centers of Islamic scholarship and culture under his protection.^193

Upon his rise to supreme power, Yusuf encountered immediate challenges from within his own family. His brothers, Ali Tegin and Ahmed, resisted his rule, with Ahmed seizing control over territories such as Balasagun, Khujand, and Ferghana, even declaring himself the Great Khan. This intra-dynastic rivalry threatened to fragment the Karakhanid state.^194

To address the growing threat, Yusuf sought an alliance with Mahmud of Ghazni, united by mutual concerns over Ali Tegin's ambitions. In a pivotal meeting in Samarkand, Yusuf and Mahmud agreed to place Transoxania under the control of Yusuf's son, Muhammad. Though initially beneficial, Mahmud's inconsistent support in countering Ali Tegin strained the alliance. Ultimately, Ali Tegin conceded to Yusuf's authority, reaffirming Yusuf's status as the paramount leader within the Karakhanid Khaganate .^195

• • •• • • • • •• • • • • • •• • • • ••• • • •••• • • ••• • • • • • • • •

Between 1025 and 1032, Yusuf and his sons captured strategic cities, including Özkent and Balasagun, the heart of the Karakhanid Khaganate. These victories consolidated Yusuf's power, forcing his brother Ahmed to recognize his supremacy, thus unifying the Karakhanid territories and stabilizing the state.^196

The Kara-Khanid ruler "Ilig Khan -Yusuf Qadir Khan" on horse, meeting with Ghaznavid Sultan Mahmud of Ghazni, who is riding an elephant, in 1017. Jami' al-tawarikh, circa 1306–1314

The alliance with Mahmud of Ghazni deteriorated over time due to Mahmud's fluctuating support. When Mahmud died in 1030 (421 AH), his son Masud sought to restore relations, sending an embassy to Yusuf with proposals for familial alliances. However, Yusuf Qadir Khan, still resentful over Ghaznavid inaction against Ali Tegin, met the envoys with a lukewarm reception in Kashgar, reflecting the fraught nature of Karakhanid-Ghaznavid relations.^197

Beyond military conquests, Yusuf's reign fostered significant cultural growth, positioning the Karakhanid state as a hub of Islamic learning. He established mosques, madrasas, and scholarly institutions, which attracted scholars from across the Islamic world. Notable figures such as Mahmud al-Kashgari and Yusuf Khass Hajib produced influential works during this period, which contributed to the legacy of Turkic and Islamic scholarship.^198 Yusuf Qadirhan's dedication to Islamic governance is encapsulated in a statement attributed to him:

> "*As far as the River Amu that is before Balkh, as far as the place called Karak on the north, I, Sultan Yusuf Qadirhan, have established the laws and religion of Muhammad, the Messenger of God, and gave them currency.*"^199

Yusuf Qadir Khan's reign marked an era of Islamic expansion within Turkic territories, laying cultural foundations that influenced the identities of later Central Asian groups. His governance elevated Kashgar as a center of learning, culture, and trade along the Silk Road, reinforcing the Karakhanid Khaganate's blend of Turkic governance and Islamic values. This blend left a lasting legacy that would inspire subsequent Central Asian states and rulers.^200

While Yusuf Qadir Khan's reign may not have achieved full consolidation of all Turkic tribes, his cultural contributions and political achievements fortified the Karakhanid state's influence. His legacy, preserved through monuments, historical texts like the *Tazkira-i Bughrakhan*, and the enduring memory of the Karakhanids, is celebrated throughout Central Asia as a testament to the power of Islamic governance and Turkic unity.

Notes

191.   *Tazkira-i Bughrakhan*; Hudud al-'Alam.

192. Sallahiat Mullah Haji, *Tazkira-i Bughrakhan*.
193. Ibid.
194. Ibn Miskawaih, *The Experiences of the Nations*; Ibn al-Athir, *The Complete History*.
195. Peter B. Golden, *An Introduction to the History of the Turkic Peoples* (Wiesbaden: Otto Harrassowitz, 1992), 214-216.
196. Michal Biran, *The Empire of the Karakhanids* (Leiden: Brill, 2005), 70-73.
197. Ibid.
198. Sallahiat Mullah Haji, *Tazkira-i Bughrakhan*.
199. Peter B. Golden, *An Introduction to the History of the Turkic Peoples* (Wiesbaden: Otto Harrassowitz, 1992), 246-248.
200. Ibid., 230-233.
201. Michal Biran, *The Empire of the Karakhanids* (Leiden: Brill, 2005), 76-78.
202. Ibid.
203. Denis Sinor, ed., *The Cambridge History of Early Inner Asia* (Cambridge: Cambridge University Press, 1990), 295-297.
204. Ibid.
205. Ibid.
206. Michal Biran, *The Empire of the Karakhanids* (Leiden: Brill, 2005), 82-84.
207. Ibid.
208. Sallahiat Mullah Haji, *Tazkira-i Bughrakhan*.
209. Michal Biran, *The Empire of the Karakhanids* (Leiden: Brill, 2005), 82-84.

Mahmud of Kashgar, also known as Kâşgarlı Mahmud, is celebrated as one of the most prominent scholars in Turkic history. His work addressed key historical and cultural challenges of his time, such as the need to preserve linguistic diversity amidst the growing dominance of Arabic and Persian, while simultaneously asserting the intellectual and cultural contributions of the Turkic world within the broader Islamic civilization. His work was groundbreaking for its time as it not only preserved the linguistic diversity of the Turkic world but also elevated the status of Turkic languages and culture within the broader Islamic civilization, bridging the gap between Arab and Turkic intellectual traditions. Born in Kashgar, a major cultural and political center within the Karakhanid Empire, Mahmud devoted his life to studying, preserving, and promoting the Turkic languages and their rich cultural heritage. His monumental work, *Dīwān Lughāt al-Turk* (Compendium of the Turkic Languages), written in the 11th century, remains an invaluable resource for understanding the Turkic world.^201

Mahmud was possibly of noble status or even a prince, as his family is thought to have been connected to the ruling Karakhanid elite. His background and position allowed him access to education and extensive travel, which were crucial for gathering the knowledge he later compiled in his *Dīwān*.

Mahmud was born around 1008–1018 CE in Kashgar, within the Karakhanid Khaganate —a Turkic state that had recently embraced Islam. Growing up in a noble family, he likely had access to high-quality education and exposure to the cultural crossroads of the Silk Road. This dynamic environment likely influenced Mahmud's lifelong dedication to documenting and celebrating Turkic languages and traditions.^202

His extensive travels across Turkic-speaking regions in Central Asia, Transoxiana, the Iranian Plateau, and the Middle East allowed him to gather linguistic and cultural material for his *Dīwān*. As he stated, "I have traveled through all the lands and steppes of the Turks, the Turkmen-Oghuz, the Chigil, the Yagma, and the Qirqiz, learning their dialects and poems. I am among the most eloquent in their language and the most articulate in expression." From the bustling bazaars of Bukhara to the scholarly hubs of Baghdad, Mahmud encountered a mosaic of cultures, languages, and traditions, which enriched his understanding of the Turkic world's diversity and its connections with neighboring civilizations. His goal was to showcase the richness and diversity of Turkic languages and emphasize the cultural and political contributions of the Turkic people to the Islamic world.^203

• ••• • • • • • • •• ••• •••• • •Dīwān Lughāt al-Turk

Mahmud had a clear purpose in writing his *Dīwān*: to preserve and elevate the Turkic language and culture. He aimed to demonstrate to the Arab world that the Turkic dialects were as sophisticated and expressive as Arabic and Persian, deserving of respect and admiration. As he stated in his *Dīwān*:

"I have written this work so that those who learn Turkish may come to know the beauty of our language and the strength of our people."^204

He presented *Dīwān Lughāt al-Turk* to the Abbasid Caliph, likely Al-Muqtadi, as a gesture of goodwill between the Turkic and Arab worlds. This act symbolized a cultural bridge, underscoring the importance of Turkic contributions to the Islamic world. By showcasing the richness of Turkic languages and traditions, Mahmud fostered mutual understanding and collaboration, further solidifying political alliances and intellectual exchanges between these civilizations. This presentation not only highlighted the intellectual and cultural depth of Turkic traditions but also reinforced the strategic alliance between the Turkic states and the Islamic Caliphate, fostering mutual respect and collaboration in governance, culture, and faith. Through this act, Mahmud sought to foster cultural respect and alliance, highlighting the Turks as essential allies and contributors to Islamic civilization.^205

16.3 • • •••• • • • ••• •• • • • ••• • • • •• •• • • • • •••• • •• ş• • ••• • • • • •••• Dīwān Lughāt al-Turk

16.3.1 Timeless Wisdom: Mahmud's Reflections on the Turkic Spirit and Values:

- On the Strength of the Turkic People: "Turks are mighty warriors; they can conquer any land and protect their own."
- On the Value of Language: "To understand a people, one must understand their language."
- Regarding Unity Among Turks: "The Turkic tribes may differ in dialect, but they are united by spirit and purpose."
- On Kashgar as a Center of Learning: "Kashgar is a beacon of knowledge, where scholars gather to share wisdom."
- On Honor and Dignity: "A Turk's dignity is his most prized possession; he will never compromise it."

- On Nomadic Life: "To wander with the herds and be free – that is the life of a true Turk."
- On Hospitality: "A guest is sacred; he brings blessings to the Turkic hearth."
- On the Value of Proverbs: "The wisdom of the elders lies in the proverbs passed down."
- On the Turkic Soul: "In every Turk, there is a flame that refuses to be extinguished."^206

16.3.2 The Pillars of Growth: Mahmud's Insights on Education, Wisdom, and Knowledge

Mahmud emphasized the importance of education, wisdom, and knowledge in his seminal work Dîvânü Lugâti't-Türk. Here are some key sayings on the subject:

- On the Value of Knowledge: "With guidance, the path is never lost; with knowledge, words are never misused."
- On the Role of the Wise: "A hero is known in the army, and a wise man in council."
- On Virtue and Wisdom: "Virtue and wisdom are the two wings that elevate a person."

These sayings reflect Mahmud's deep respect for education and his belief in the vital role of wisdom in individual and societal growth.

16.3.3 His Views on Turks, Uyghurs, and Other Turkic Tribes
16.3.3.1   Turks

Mahmud expressed a profound pride in his Turkic heritage, regarding the Turkic language as equal to or even superior to other languages of the Islamic world. His assertions not only elevated the status of Turkic languages but also challenged contemporary linguistic hierarchies within the Islamic world, earning him respect among Arab and Persian scholars who recognized the cultural and political significance of the Turkic peoples. He portrayed the Turks as a strong and noble people, favored by God and essential as warriors and administrators. He famously wrote:

- "God has created the Turks with greatness and bestowed justice upon them."
- "The Turks are a people of valor, who ride like the wind and fight like thunder."
- "Turks value honor above all, for without honor, a man is as a body without a soul."

- "Among the Turks, hospitality is revered; a guest is akin to a gift from heaven."
- "The language of the Turk is as boundless as their lands and as rich as their heritage."
- "Bravery flows through the blood of the Turks as surely as rivers to the sea."
- "The Turks respect wisdom and value age, for in the elders lies the wisdom of the past."
- "For the Turk, loyalty is sacred, and a promise is kept even at great personal cost."
- "Turks do not flee from the battlefield; to them, honor in death is the highest reward."
- "The strength of the Turk lies not only in his arms but in his unwavering spirit."
- "The Turk lives with pride in his heritage, carrying the legacy of his ancestors forward."[207]

16.3.3.2 Uyghurs

Mahmud had complex views on the Uyghurs. While he recognized their significant cultural contributions, he was critical of their pre-Islamic religious practices, particularly Manichaeism, which he saw as a period of moral decline. Nonetheless, he respected their achievements in literature and administration, documenting Uyghur words in his *Dīwān* and valuing their linguistic uniqueness within the Turkic family. His quotes about the Uyghurs from *Dīwān Lughāt al-Turk* include:

- "There are still some words in the Uyghur language that carry traces of their pre-Islamic past."
- "The Uyghurs excel in diplomacy, securing peace even in times of unrest."
- "The Uyghurs distinguish themselves from other Turkic tribes through their knowledge and script."
- "The Uyghurs are masters of trade, their merchants skilled in the arts of negotiation."
- "Among the Uyghurs, wisdom flows like water; they value learning and culture."
- "The Uyghurs are a people of poetry, and their words carry the weight of their rich history."
- "Uyghur lands are where the arts flourish, for they are both guardians and creators of beauty."[208]

16.3.3.3 Quotes about the Oghuz, Kipchak, and Karluk Tribes

1. "The Oghuz are warriors, known for their skill in battle and loyalty to their leaders."
2. "The Kipchaks, though fierce, are fair and just in their dealings with others."
3. "Among the Karluks, family ties are sacred, and kinship binds them like iron."
4. "Oghuz warriors are as swift as falcons, striking fear into the hearts of their enemies."

5. "The Karluks hold their honor dear, living by codes passed down through generations."

16.3.3.4 Kashgar: The Pride of the Turkic World

Mahmud took immense pride in his homeland and capital of the Karakhanid Khaganate, Kashgar, which he considered a cultural and intellectual hub of the Turkic world. To him, Kashgar symbolized the preservation of the Turkic language and culture in its purest form, embodying the union of Turkic martial spirit with the intellectual and spiritual depth of Islam.

- "Kashgar is the crown of Turkistan, a city where learning and trade flourish hand in hand."
- "Kashgar is the jewel of the Turkic lands; it is the city of scholars and artisans."
- "Among the Turks, Kashgar is where the language is spoken most beautifully."
- "Kashgar is the destination for those who seek knowledge."
- "Everyone from Kashgar adheres to Turkic traditions."[209]

• • •• • • • • • • • • •• • ••• • • ••• • •

Mahmud's *Dīwān Lughāt al-Turk* served as both a dictionary and an ethnographic study, introducing the Arabic-speaking world to the richness of Turkic languages and cultures. He compiled proverbs, poetry, and sayings from various Turkic tribes, including the Oghuz, Karluks, and Kipchaks, preserving invaluable insights into Turkic values, beliefs, and daily life. One of his famous proverbs states:

"The word of a Turk is sharper than a sword."[210]

Life and Scholarship of Mahmud of Kashgar

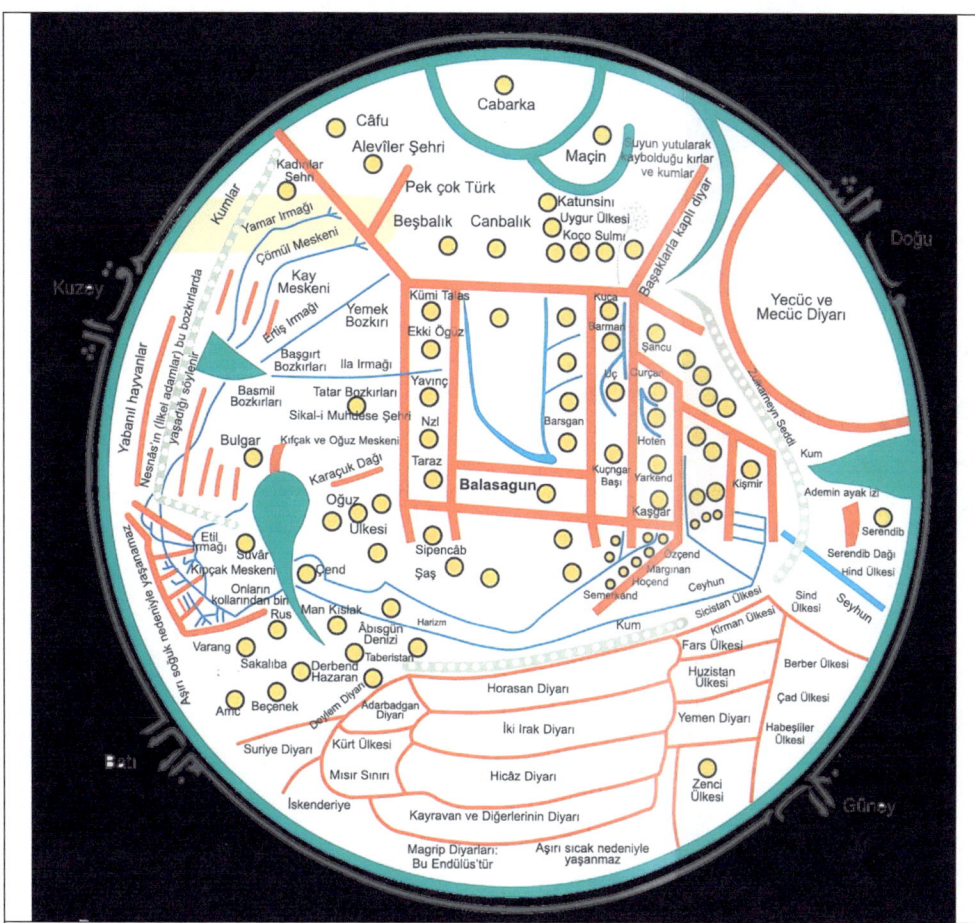

Modern Turkish translation of Mahmud Kashgari's 11th-century world map, featured in his *Diwan Lughat al-Turk*, one of the earliest maps centered on the Turkic world, reflecting the era's geographic knowledge and cultural connections.

• •• • •• • •• •

Mahmud's life and work are a testament to his deep pride in the Turkic people and their heritage. His efforts laid the groundwork for modern studies of Turkic languages and culture, inspiring scholars to further explore the linguistic, historical, and cultural significance of the Turkic world. Through his pioneering scholarship, Mahmud continues to influence contemporary understanding of Central Asia's rich legacy and its contributions to global civilization. His *Dīwān Lughāt al-Turk* stands as a historical record of Turkic linguistic, cultural, and intellectual achievements, showcasing the contributions of diverse Turkic groups, including the Uyghurs. Through this work, Mahmud highlighted the Turks' role as defenders of Islam and champions of justice, celebrating Kashgar as a thriving center of Turkic civilization within the broader Islamic world. The legacy of the Karakhanid language, strengthened by Mahmud's scholarship, played a pivotal role in shaping the linguistic and cultural identity of Central Asia, leaving a lasting impact on subsequent Turkic states.^211

Notes

201. Michal Biran, *The Empire of the Karakhanids* (Leiden: Brill, 2005).
202. Ibid.
203. Ibid.
204. Mahmud al-Kashgari, *Dīwān Lughāt al-Turk* (Istanbul: Maarif Matbaasi, 1915).
205. Ibid.
206. Ibid.
207. Mahmud al-Kashgari, *Dīwān Lughāt al-Turk*.
208. Ibid.
209. Ibid.
210. Ibid.
211. Michal Biran, *The Empire of the Karakhanids*.

Yusuf Has Hajib: A Visionary of Governance and Moral Philosophy

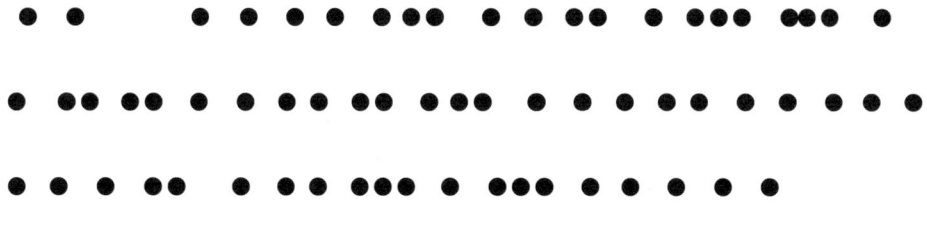

Yusuf Has Hajib, a prominent Uyghur scholar, poet, and statesman from the 11th century, is celebrated for his influential work, *Kutadgu Bilig* ("The Wisdom of Royal Glory"). Born around 1018 in Balasagun, a city under the Karakhanid Empire (now modern-day Kyrgyzstan), Yusuf dedicated his life to scholarship, with a strong focus on governance, ethics, and social justice. His work emphasizes the virtues of a just ruler, the power of knowledge, and the moral responsibilities of leadership. Written in the context of Islamic philosophy and Central Asian values, *Kutadgu Bilig* offers a profound guide on governing with integrity and achieving balance in life.^212

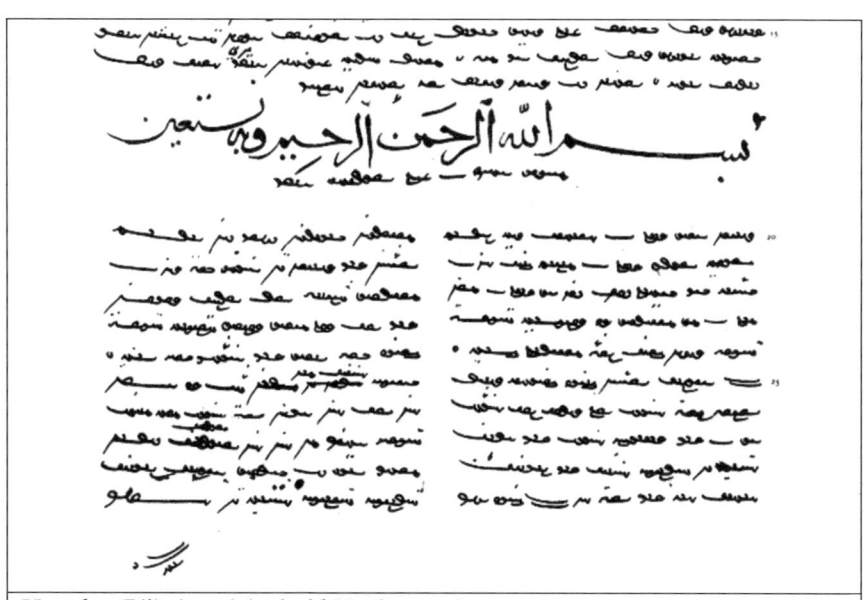

Kutadgu Bilig in original old Uyghur script. Source: W. Radloff. St. Petersburg : J. Glasunof und Eggers, 1891-1910. p.10.

Around 1070, Yusuf completed *Kutadgu Bilig* in Kashgar, the capital and a major cultural center of the Karakhanid Empire. He dedicated his work to Sultan Tavghach Bughra Khan, the ruler of the empire, who, impressed by Yusuf's wisdom, awarded him the honorary title of "Has Hajib" (Chief Chamberlain or Advisor). Through his esteemed role at court, Yusuf's legacy extended beyond his lifetime, as his insights into governance, justice, and ethical leadership continued to influence generations.

Yusuf Has Hajib's writings are filled with timeless wisdom on virtues, learning, leadership, family, and early education. Below are some of his most insightful quotes:

17.2.1 On Life and Virtues

- "Wisdom is a torch; it is the eye for the blind, the soul for the lifeless body, and words for the speechless."
- "Those born will die, and from them remains only their words. Speak wisely, and you shall live forever."
- "The arrogant and boastful man becomes tasteless and disliked; the proud man's honor fades day by day."
- "A person's value lies in his words; one rises or falls by the tongue."
- "The virtuous man covers the faults of others; the wicked man seeks them out."

17.2.2 On the Value of Learning

- "Knowledge is like a treasure chest; the more you have, the richer you become, and no one can steal it from you."
- "Learning refines a person's character, just as a sculptor carves beauty from stone."
- "The path to wisdom is paved with knowledge; without learning, one wanders aimlessly in darkness."
- "Seek knowledge as if it is food for the soul; for a wise mind, learning is never enough."
- "A person without knowledge is like a tree without roots; it may stand for a while, but it withers quickly."

17.2.3 On the Importance of Knowledge

- "Knowledge is the crown of the wise; without it, one cannot see the path ahead."

- "A person with knowledge is like a beacon in the darkness, illuminating the way for others."
- "True wealth is found in knowledge, for riches can fade, but wisdom endures forever."
- "A mind filled with knowledge is a fortress that no enemy can conquer."
- "The pursuit of knowledge is the highest duty of man; through it, he elevates both himself and those around him."

17.2.4 On Leadership and Unity

- "A good leader is one who listens to the wisdom of others, for no one can carry the weight of governance alone."
- "Justice is the foundation of leadership; a ruler must be as fair as the scales, and his people will unite under his rule."
- "The wise leader knows that strength lies in unity. When the people are united, the nation stands firm."
- "A true leader serves as a shelter for his people; just as the sun spreads warmth to all, so must a ruler spread care to his people."
- "When there is harmony among the people and their leader, prosperity flows, and peace prevails."

17.2.5 On Family and Early Education

- "Teach a child the ways of wisdom from an early age, for a sapling grows strong only if guided properly from the start."
- "A child who learns respect for family and elders in his youth grows into a person who respects all."
- "Parents are the first teachers; through them, a child learns honor, patience, and kindness."
- "The habits formed in youth last a lifetime; nurture a child's character with love and guidance, for it shapes his entire life."
- "In a harmonious family, wisdom flourishes; teach children early, for they are the future caretakers of virtue."

17.2.6 Additional Quotes from Kutadgu Bilig

1. "Seek wisdom, for it will guard you when wealth cannot."
2. "A ruler without justice is like a bird without wings."
3. "The wealth of a country lies in the education of its people."
4. "Where there is no knowledge, there can be no wisdom, and where there is no wisdom, life cannot flourish."
5. "Compassion and justice must walk hand in hand, for only then will peace reign."

6. "Do not boast of wealth, for wisdom is the true treasure that outlasts all riches."
7. "Patience and resilience are the hallmarks of a strong mind."
8. "The leader who fails to protect his people fails to rule."
9. "Respect others' worth and show kindness in all dealings."
10. "A wise word is like a sword—it cuts through ignorance and defends the truth."
11. "Greatness is not in power but in the integrity of one's actions."
12. "True beauty lies in the character of a person, not in their appearance."
13. "To preserve peace, a wise leader tempers justice with mercy."
14. "A good leader listens to the grievances of his people and serves them with humility."
15. "Fortune favors the brave, but only wisdom can sustain them."
16. "Do not let anger cloud your judgment; it destroys even the wisest of men."
17. "A kingdom without justice is like a tree without roots—it cannot stand."
18. "Education is a lamp that guides even the most troubled souls toward truth."
19. "One cannot lead without first mastering self-discipline and respect."
20. "Seek knowledge not just for yourself but to uplift your community."

This collection of quotes and insights reflects the timeless wisdom and guidance in *Kutadgu Bilig*, a work that continues to shape discussions on ethics, leadership, and the values that sustain communities across generations.^214

• • •• •• • • • • •• ••• • • • ••• • • •• • •••

Yusuf Has Hajib's legacy extends beyond his lifetime, with *Kutadgu Bilig* continuing to inspire with its insights into justice, leadership, knowledge, and moral conduct. Modern scholars have appraised his work as a cornerstone of Turkish-Islamic literature, noting its profound influence on both governance and ethical thought. Historian Robert Dankoff, for instance, highlights its unique synthesis of Central Asian traditions and Islamic values, underscoring its relevance across diverse cultural contexts. Revered as one of the earliest examples of Turkic-Islamic literature, the work has become a model for ethical governance, encouraging rulers and individuals alike to prioritize wisdom and justice. The enduring popularity of *Kutadgu Bilig* in Turkish and Central Asian scholarship underscores Yusuf's lasting impact, with his principles echoing in discussions on leadership, learning, and societal well-being to this day. His emphasis on knowledge, unity, family, and integrity remains as relevant now as it was nearly a thousand years ago.^215

Notes

212. Michal Biran, *The Empire of the Karakhanids* (Leiden: Brill, 2005).
213. Ibid.

214. Yusuf Has Hajib, *Kutadgu Bilig*, trans. Robert Dankoff (Albany: SUNY Press, 1983).
215. Ibid.

From Empires to Exile: A Brief Uyghur History

The Karakhanid Khaganate, which ruled parts of Central Asia from the 10th to the 12th centuries, was not only a powerful political entity but also a pioneering force in shaping Turkic civilization. Through their governance, cultural initiatives, and embrace of Islam, the Karakhanids laid a foundation that profoundly influenced subsequent Turkic empires and tribes, including the Oghuz and Kipchaq. This chapter explores the Karakhanids' enduring legacy across governance, language, religion, culture, and their impact on neighboring Turkic groups.

The Karakhanids were among the first Turkic dynasties to adopt Islam as the state religion, a decision that dramatically transformed their governance. By integrating Islamic principles with Turkic tribal structures, the Karakhanids pioneered a model of rule that emphasized justice, unity, and religious devotion.^216 This hybrid governance model attracted loyalty from various Turkic tribes, promoting internal cohesion and stability. It served as a template for later Turkic-Islamic states, notably the Seljuk Empire.^217

Their administration was highly organized, balancing central authority with tribal autonomy—a feature that appealed to other Turkic groups accustomed to clan-based leadership. By demonstrating that Islamic law could harmonize with Turkic traditions, the Karakhanids fostered a shared vision of a Turkic-Islamic civilization.^218

The Karakhanids' conversion to Islam was a pivotal moment in Turkic history. By officially adopting the religion, they facilitated its spread across Central Asia, influencing neighboring tribes and reinforcing a spiritual bond among Turkic peoples. They actively promoted Islamic teachings, constructing mosques, madrasas, and centers for scholarship, particularly in Kashgar, which became a hub of Islamic learning.^219

Their efforts in harmonizing Turkic traditions with Islamic practices created a cultural identity that resonated with other tribes, including the Oghuz and Kipchaq. The Oghuz, who later formed the Seljuk Empire, adopted similar governance structures, while the Kipchaq began incorporating Islamic customs through interactions with Muslim states.

79

This Islamization unified Central Asia, laying the groundwork for a Turkic-Islamic civilization.[220]

• • •• • • • •• •• • • ••• • •• ••• • • • •• ••• • • • • • • •• • • •• ••• • • • ••

   The Karakhanids elevated the Turkic language, known as "Türkche" or "Türkî," to a prominent status in administration, literature, and religious discourse. While Persian and Arabic dominated the Islamic world, the Karakhanids used Turkic for state documents, literature, and Islamic scholarship, thereby legitimizing it as a refined language.[221]

   This linguistic elevation was epitomized by two seminal works: *Kutadgu Bilig* by Yusuf Khass Hajib and *Diwan Lughat al-Turk* by Mahmud al-Kashghari. Yusuf Khass Hajib's treatise emphasized ethics and governance, while Kashghari's ethnographic dictionary preserved Turkic dialects and celebrated their richness. Kashghari remarked, "Know that the Turkic language is as precious as the Persian tongue," underscoring the cultural pride of the era. These works inspired neighboring Turkic groups, such as the Oghuz, to adopt Turkic as a literary and cultural medium, reinforcing a shared linguistic heritage.[222]

   The Karakhanid language laid the foundation for the common Turkish literary language that later came to be known as Chaghatay. Scholars such as Marcel Erdal and Gerard Clauson highlight the Karakhanid period as a pivotal era that established the groundwork for subsequent Turkic literary traditions, including Chaghatay. The Karakhanid era introduced a rich vocabulary, sophisticated syntactic structures, and enduring literary themes, which were later inherited and refined by Chaghatay authors, most notably Ali-Shir Nava'i, who elevated the language to new artistic and cultural heights.

• • •• • • ••• •• ••• • • • • • • • ••• • •• •• • ••• •• • • •• ••• • • • • ••

   Under the Karakhanids, Kashgar became a cultural and educational center. The Khaganate invested in institutions that fostered scholarship in theology, poetry, history, and science. Scholars from across Central Asia and beyond were drawn to Kashgar, creating a cosmopolitan atmosphere where Turkic and Islamic traditions merged.[223] This cultural flowering solidified Kashgar's status as a beacon of Turkic-Islamic civilization.[224]

   The Karakhanids' support for education and the arts inspired later Turkic leaders, who emulated their cultural policies. Their efforts preserved Turkic heritage while integrating it into the broader Islamic world, producing a rich synthesis of ideas and traditions.

• • •• •• ••• • • • • •• • ••• • • •• • • • • •• • ••• • •• •• • •• ••• • ••• • ••

The Karakhanids provided a model for the Oghuz Turks, who transitioned from a nomadic lifestyle to forming the Seljuk Empire. Observing the Karakhanid synthesis of Turkic governance with Islamic values, the Oghuz adopted and adapted these principles. The Seljuks further promoted Turkic as an administrative language, continuing the Karakhanid legacy of cultural and linguistic pride.^225

The Seljuks also inherited the Karakhanids' role as protectors of Islamic civilization, fostering unity and leadership within the Turkic-Islamic world. This cultural continuity reinforced a shared identity that spanned Central Asia and the Middle East.^226

The Kipchaq Turks, though largely independent, were influenced by the Karakhanids through cultural exchanges and trade. Proximity to Karakhanid lands introduced Islamic practices and Turkic-Islamic customs to the Kipchaq, strengthening a shared heritage among Turkic tribes.^227 Ahmad Yasawi, a 12th-century Turkic Sufi poet, significantly influenced the spiritual landscape of Turkic-speaking peoples, including the Kipchaq Turks. His seminal work, *Diwan-i Hikmet* (*Book of Wisdom*), was composed in a Turkic language accessible to various Turkic tribes, facilitating the dissemination of his Sufi teachings across Central Asia. This linguistic approach enabled nomadic groups like the Kipchaq to engage with Islamic spirituality in their native tongue, fostering a deeper cultural and religious connection.This integration furthered the spread of Turkic-Islamic culture across Central Asia and into Eastern Europe.^228

Notes

216. Peter B. Golden, *Central Asia in World History* (Oxford: Oxford University Press, 2011).
217. Denis Sinor, ed., *The Cambridge History of Early Inner Asia* (Cambridge: Cambridge University Press, 1990).
218. Peter B. Golden, *An Introduction to the History of the Turkic Peoples* (Wiesbaden: Harrassowitz, 1992).
219. Richard Foltz, *Religions of the Silk Road* (New York: Palgrave Macmillan, 2010).
220. Peter B. Golden, *The Turkic World* (London: Routledge, 2007).
221. Golden, *An Introduction to the History of the Turkic Peoples*.
222. Ibid.
223. Klaus Zieme, "The Karakhanid Epoch and Its Role in the Cultural Development of Central Asia," in *History of Civilizations of Central Asia*, ed. Dani Masson (Paris: UNESCO, 2002).
224. Ivan Ecsedy, "The Cultural Legacy of the Karakhanids," *Central Asiatic Journal* 50, no. 1 (2006): 45-60.
225. Clifford Edmund Bosworth, *The Ghaznavids: Their Empire in Afghanistan and Eastern Iran* (Edinburgh: Edinburgh University Press, 1996).

226. Richard N. Frye, *The Heritage of Central Asia: From Antiquity to the Turkish Expansion* (Princeton: Markus Wiener Publishers, 1996).
227. Golden, *The Turkic World*.
228. Devin DeWeese, *Islamization and Native Religion in the Golden Horde* (University Park: Pennsylvania State University Press, 1994).

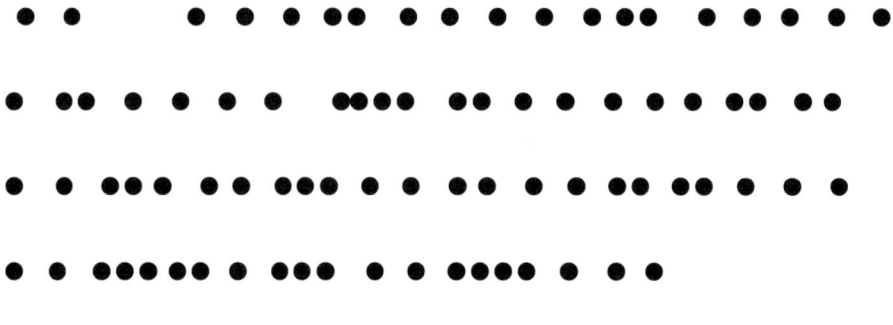

The Uyghur Qocho Kingdom, known internally as the Idiqut Kingdom (meaning "Holy Majesty" or "Sacred Lord" in Turkic) by its own rulers, was established in the mid-9th century. The term "Idiqut" signified both reverence and divine authority and was written in Old Uyghur as "𐰖𐰑𐰴𐰆𐱃." This kingdom was also called Kara-Khoja. Externally, the Qocho Kingdom was known by various names: Chinese sources referred to it as the "Huigu Gaochang Kingdom" indicating its Uyghur identity and governance over the region of Gaochang (modern-day Turpan). Islamic sources, especially Arab and Persian historians, often called it "the Uyghur Kingdom of Qocho" and described it as a Buddhist kingdom due to its strong religious identity distinct from the Islamic world.^229

The establishment of the Uyghur Qocho Kingdom marked a revival of the Uyghur imperial legacy rather than a mere continuation. Officially established around 843 CE, the kingdom centered its governance in Qocho (known in modern-day as Turpan), which served as its capital. Following the fall of the Uyghur Khaganate in Mongolia in 840 CE, brought about by Kirghiz raids, the Ediz tribe, including its ruling members, sought refuge and reorganized among the scattered Uyghur tribes. The territories of the Qocho Kingdom extended northward beyond the Tengri Mountains, eastward toward Kumul, southward deep into the Tarim Basin, and westward to Kucha and Aksu, cementing its role as a significant power in Central Asia.

The migration and establishment of the kingdom, guided by Pan Tekin, marked the beginning of the Uyghurs' transition to a settled and culturally sophisticated society in the Tarim Basin. Under Pan Tekin's leadership, the kingdom thrived as a cultural and economic hub, embracing Buddhism, Manichaeism, and other religions, while developing agriculture and fostering trade with neighboring powers like China. The new state's foundation and governance were shaped by the tribal confederation structure of the Toquz Oghuz, with the Ediz tribe playing a crucial role in the westward migration and early organization of the Qocho state, alongside remnants of other Toquz Oghuz tribes.^230 This new state not only preserved Uyghur traditions but also adapted to its new environment, ensuring the survival and prosperity of the Uyghur people in the Tarim Basin.

The Uyghur migration was not an aimless journey. These tribes moved with purpose, traversing the steppes of Mongolia and passing through territories that had once been under their control, such as the Orkhon Valley and the Altai Mountains. They followed the ancient caravan routes they had once patrolled, stopping at oases and trade posts that had been under the protection of the Uyghur Khagans.^232

Before the establishment of the Uyghur Kingdom of Qocho, the region already had a deep-rooted Turkic presence. Various Turkic groups, including the Tiele and the Göktürk Khaganate, historically originated from and considered these areas, as their homeland. During the Tang Empire's temporary conquests into Turkistan, the Tang administration relied on local Turkic generals, such as Ashina She'er, to maintain control and protect the Silk Road.^233 As they settled in the Tarim Basin, the Uyghurs assimilated with local Turkic populations and other resident groups, fostering a culturally rich society that integrated Buddhist, Sogdian, Tocharian, Chinese, and other regional influences. The Uyghurs blended their nomadic Turkic heritage with a settled oasis lifestyle, creating a hybrid culture characterized by diverse religious and cultural traditions, including Buddhism, Manichaeism, Nestorian Christianity, and Tengriism. This coexistence of faiths and ethnicities fostered a rich cultural heritage, making Qocho a center of trade, art, and learning along the Silk Road while integrating elements from China, Persia, and India.^234

The Uyghur Qocho Kingdom's governance structure and tribal affiliations were firmly rooted in the alliances that had underpinned the old Uyghur Khaganate. Even after their migration to the Tarim Basin, the Uyghurs continued to identify as part of the Toquz Oghuz, maintaining unity under this ancestral framework.^235

The Uyghur Qocho Kingdom is celebrated not only for its political resilience but for its cultural and intellectual contributions to Central Asian civilization. The Uyghurs continued to use their script, derived from the Sogdian alphabet, which later influenced the Mongol and Manchu scripts. Persian historian Gardizi noted the Uyghur rulers' high regard for literacy and culture, an uncommon trait among Turkic leaders of the period. Under the Uyghurs, this script became a tool for cultural preservation and literary development, fostering a rich written tradition.^236

The adaptation of woodblock printing in Qocho also promoted the spread of Buddhist texts, contributing to Qocho's reputation as a religious and cultural hub. Buddhist texts, such as the illustrated *Maitrisimit*, were transcribed and disseminated from Qocho, reflecting the Uyghurs' dedication to Buddhist teachings.^237

• • •• • • •• ••• •• •••• •• • • • •• • •• • ••• • •• • • • • • •• ••• ••• • • • •

The Uyghur Qocho Kingdom served as a major trading hub on the Silk Road, facilitating connections between East and West through extensive commercial networks. Persian geographer Al-Istakhri described the Uyghur capital of Qocho as "a splendid city where merchants from many lands gather," underscoring its prosperity and strategic location on the Silk Road.^238 This prominence enabled the Uyghurs to maintain economic and cultural links with neighboring regions, enhancing their influence across Central Asia.

The Khaganate's oasis agriculture was highly developed, supporting a wide range of crops and livestock that sustained the local population and passing merchants alike. Chinese sources praised the kingdom's *"lush fields and abundant fruit,"* especially its grapes and melons, which became renowned throughout the region.^239 The fertile lands and advanced irrigation systems established Qocho as a self-sufficient and agriculturally productive center, contributing further to its economic vitality and attraction as a trade hub.

• • •• • • ••• •• • ••• • •• • • • • • • •• • • •• • • • • ••• •

The Uyghur Qocho Kingdom was notable for its religious tolerance, embracing Buddhism, Manichaeism, Nestorian Christianity, and later, Islam. Uyghur rulers allowed these various religious communities to coexist, creating a society enriched by interfaith exchanges. This tolerance fostered an environment in which Uyghur art, literature, and religious thought could thrive, producing an influential Uyghur identity that blended Turkic and regional cultural elements.^240

The Uyghur Qocho Kingdom: A Legacy of Cultural Synthesis and Political Resilience

Painting of Buddhist monks from the Eastern Tarim basin, Bezelek, c. 8th century AD

Manichean scribes from Qocho, 8th–9th century

> Bezeklik caves near Turpan, contains buddhist paintings; source: ((FileUpload Bot (Colegota) is licensed under CC BY-SA 4.0. Source: Wikimedia Commons.

• • •• • •• •• • • • • •• • • •• • •••• • ••• •••• • • • •

Wang Yandi, a Tang scholar who visited the Uyghurs, praised them as *"a civilized and orderly nation that had successfully merged Turkic nomadic traditions with settled Chinese practices. Their cities reflected a harmonious blend of steppe vitality and the refined aesthetics of Chinese architecture. The Uyghur Khagan was a man of great learning, known to discuss Buddhist sutras and Confucian classics with equal expertise. Markets in Gaochang thrived with the presence of merchants from diverse regions, including Khitan, Sogdian, Persian, and Arab traders, operating under the strict yet fair laws of the Khagan. Festivals of music and dance frequently filled the courtyards of their temples, showcasing the Uyghur people's deep love for culture and the arts"*.^241

Arab historian Al-Muqaddasi referred to the Uyghurs as "*wise rulers of the northern lands*" and highlighted their adeptness at fostering stability and prosperity in their domain. He remarked on their justice, organization, and their vital role in maintaining a realm where trade and cultural exchange flourished. Al-Muqaddasi wrote,

"*The Uyghurs govern with remarkable wisdom, ensuring safety along trade routes and extending hospitality to merchants and travelers from far and wide. Their leaders are known for their justice and skill in diplomacy, maintaining a realm where diverse cultures and religions coexist peacefully.*" He further noted their influence in facilitating regional trade networks and cultural exchanges. Despite religious differences, the Uyghurs maintained peaceful relations with their Islamic neighbors, skillfully navigating diplomatic ties and commercial alliances to enhance mutual prosperity.^242

Notes

229. Michal Biran, *The Empire of the Karakhanids* (Leiden: Brill, 2005).
230. Peter B. Golden, *An Introduction to the History of the Turkic Peoples* (Wiesbaden: Harrassowitz, 1992).
231. Ibid.
232. Ibid.
233. Denis Sinor, ed., *The Cambridge History of Early Inner Asia* (Cambridge: Cambridge University Press, 1990).
234. Biran, *The Empire of the Karakhanids*, 2005.
235. Ibid.
236. Ibid.

237. Wang Yandi, *Tang Huiyao*.
238. Al-Istakhri, *Kitab al-Masalik wa'l-Mamalik*.
239. Wang Yandi, *Tang Huiyao*.
240. Biran, *The Empire of the Karakhanids*, 2005.
241. Denis Sinor, ed., *The Cambridge History of Early Inner Asia* (Cambridge: Cambridge University Press, 1990).
242. Al-Muqaddasi, *Ahsan al-Taqasim fi Ma'rifat al-Aqalim*.

From Empires to Exile: A Brief Uyghur History

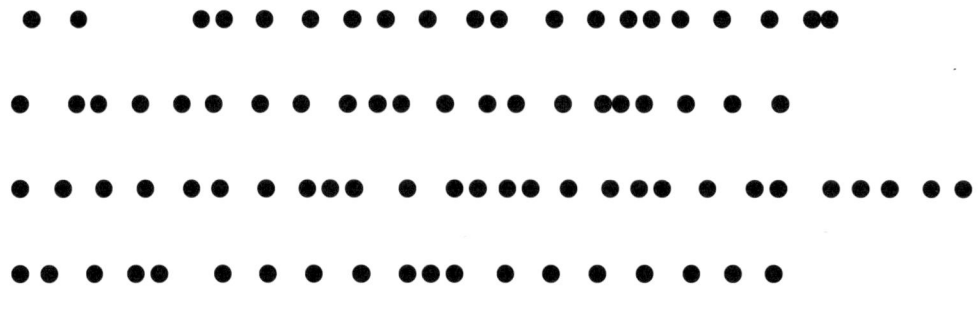

The origins of both the Qocho Kingdom and the Karakhanid Khaganate lineages intersect through the Toquz Oghuz confederation and other Turkic tribes that formed the foundation of the early Uyghur Khaganate. Following the Khaganate's collapse in 840 CE, the tribes diverged: some migrated to the Tarim Basin, where they established the Qocho Kingdom, while others, notably the Karluks and Yaghma, migrated westward to establish the Karakhanid Khaganate.^242

The Karakhanid Khaganate converted to Islam by the 10th century, marking a religious and cultural departure from the Qocho Kingdom, which adhered to Buddhism and Manichaeism. This religious distinction forged two unique cultural paths: the Karakhanids became an Islamic power with strong scholarly traditions, while the Qocho Kingdom flourished as a Buddhist cultural center on the Silk Road.^243

By the late 10th century, the Karakhanid Khaganate sought to extend its influence eastward, eyeing the prosperous oasis cities of the Tarim Basin, including Turpan and Kucha. The Karakhanid ruler Yusuf Qadir Khan led campaigns in 1017 that pushed as far northeast as Beshbaliq, a significant city within the Qocho Kingdom's territory. However, the Qocho Kingdom effectively utilized its geographic position to defend key areas, preserving its autonomy and religious identity. Realizing the logistical difficulties of maintaining control over these distant regions, the Karakhanids ultimately reached informal agreements with the Qocho Kingdom, establishing Kucha as a buffer zone. This period of coexistence enabled both sides to benefit from stable Silk Road trade, promoting mutual economic cooperation.^244

Shared Heritage, Divergent Paths, and Eventual Unification After the Mongol Conquest

By the mid-11th century, internal divisions weakened the Karakhanid Khaganate, while the Qocho Kingdom continued to flourish as a Buddhist center. Although Islam began to spread gradually in parts of the Tarim Basin, both khaganates retained their cultural identities amidst Central Asia's shifting political landscape. However, the arrival of the Mongol Empire in the 13th century dramatically altered this balance.

The Karakhanid Khaganate faced its downfall through a series of conquests between 1211 and 1218 CE. In 1212, the last Western Karakhanid ruler, Sultan Uthman, supported a rebellion in Samarkand but was executed when Khwarezm-Shah Muhammad retaliated, ending Karakhanid rule in the west. Meanwhile, Eastern Karakhanid power was overthrown by Kuchlug, a Naiman prince who seized control in 1211. By 1218, as the Mongols advanced, they defeated Kuchlug, whose religious restrictions had caused unrest in Kashgar. The Mongols promised religious freedom, gaining local support, and integrated the region into their empire.^245

As the Mongols consolidated their power, the Mongols dismantled the Karakhanid Khaganate and incorporated the Qocho Kingdom as a vassal state, granting it limited autonomy.^245 Under the Chagatai Khanate, founded by Genghis Khan's descendants, a unique cultural synthesis emerged. The Chagatai rulers encouraged the coexistence of Buddhist and Islamic practices, fostering a more cohesive regional identity that bridged previously divided Turkic groups. During this period, the Mongol administration saw a gradual reduction in the prominence of the Uyghur name in official contexts, categorizing subjects broadly based on tribal and administrative divisions. Despite this, the Qocho Uyghurs retained their distinct identity, often being referred to both as "Uyghurs" and broadly as "Turks," reflecting their Turkic heritage and historical association with the Uyghur name. This Mongol influence cultivated a rich cultural landscape in East Turkistan, where Uyghur Buddhism and Turkic Islam coexisted, enriching the region's diversity.^246

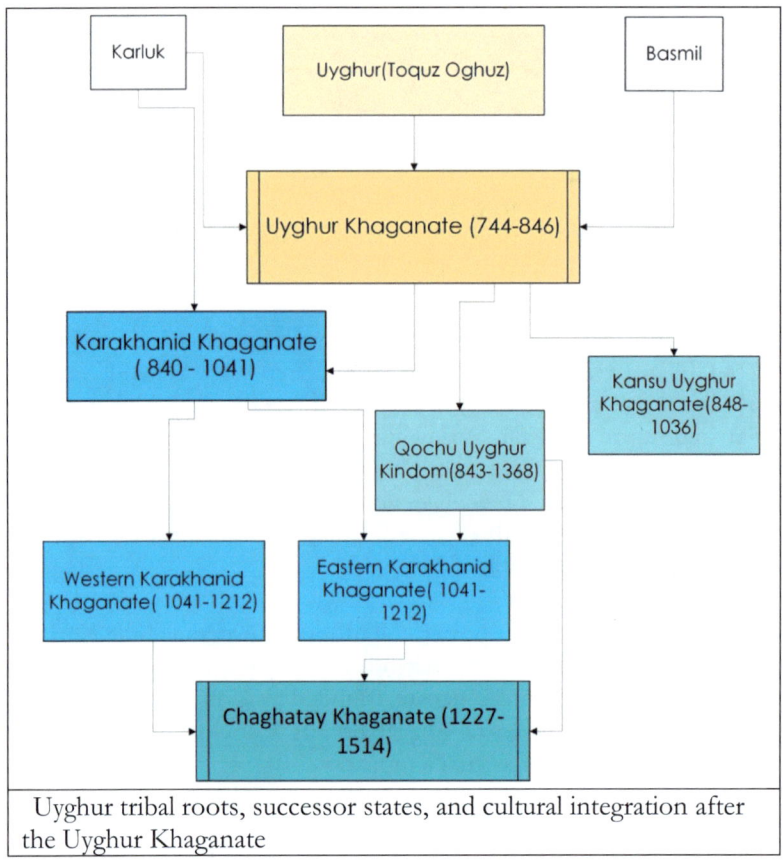

Uyghur tribal roots, successor states, and cultural integration after the Uyghur Khaganate

By the 15th and 16th centuries, Islam had become the dominant religion in the Tarim Basin, with the last remaining Buddhist and non-Muslim Uyghur communities adopting Islam. This transformation was influenced by the legacy of Karakhanid culture and the support of later Islamic rulers, who recognized the Uyghur population's role in consolidating regional religious authority. The unification under Islam, facilitated by both Mongol influence and successive Muslim dynasties, fostered a shared Uyghur identity that blended Turkic heritage, Buddhist past, and Islamic traditions.

This convergence of the Karakhanid and Qocho cultural legacies laid the foundation for an enduring Uyghur identity that remains culturally significant in the region today.^247

Notes

242. Peter B. Golden, *An Introduction to the History of the Turkic Peoples* (Wiesbaden: Harrassowitz, 1992), pp. 214-217.
243. Michal Biran, *The Empire of the Karakhanids* (Leiden: Brill, 2005), pp. 70-73.
244. Denis Sinor, ed., *The Cambridge History of Early Inner Asia* (Cambridge: Cambridge University Press, 1990), pp. 310-315.
245. David Morgan, *The Mongols* (Oxford: Blackwell, 1991), pp. 50-52.
246. Biran, *The Empire of the Karakhanids*, 2005, pp. 93-96.
247. Ibid., pp. 97-100.

From Empires to Exile: A Brief Uyghur History

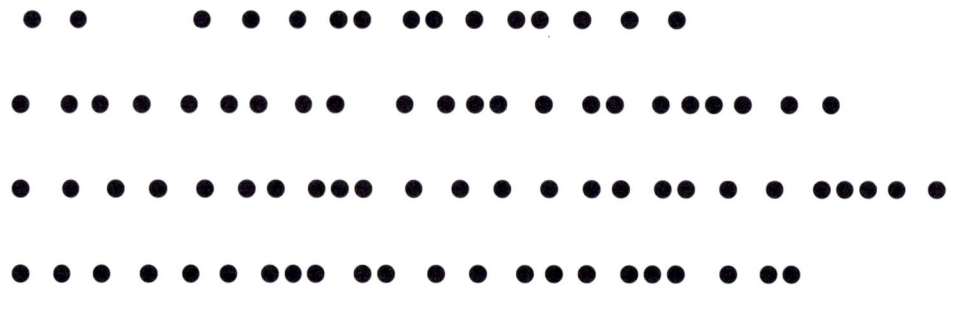

The Mongol Empire, led by Genghis Khan, began its westward expansion in 1209 CE, targeting the prosperous Uyghur Qocho Kingdom in the Tarim Basin. Recognizing the futility of resisting, Uyghur Khagan Barchuk Art Tekin opted for voluntary submission. According to the Yuan Shi, the official history of the Yuan Empire, Barchuk declared, "The wisdom of Genghis Khan is like the wisdom of the sky itself. We, the people of the Uyghur, seek to serve the Great Khan." Genghis Khan accepted this loyalty and appointed Barchuk Art Tekin as a vassal king, granting the Uyghurs autonomy to govern their lands. Additionally, Genghis Khan declared Barchuk as his "fifth son" and strengthened the alliance through a marriage, giving his daughter Altun Begi to Barchuk in wedlock. Uyghur officials were incorporated into the Mongol administration as scribes, governors, and advisors, and the Uyghur script was adopted as the official script of the Mongol Empire. ^248

After Genghis Khan's death in 1227 CE, his empire was divided among his sons. Central Asia, including the former Uyghur and Karakhanid territories, was allocated to his second son, Chagatai, marking the birth of the Chagatai Khanate. The Chagatai Khanate, founded in the early 13th century, stretched across Central Asia from the Altai Mountains in the east to the Oxus River (Amu Darya) in the west, covering much of present-day East Turkistan, Uzbekistan, Kyrgyzstan, and parts of Kazakhstan and Tajikistan. ^249

The capital of the Chagatai Khanate initially shifted between key cities like Almaliq (in modern Ghulja) and later Samarkand, depending on the ruling khan and political stability within the region. Almaliq, located in what is now the Ili River Valley, was particularly significant for the eastern Chagatai rulers, while Samarkand became the cultural heart of the western Chagatai lands, especially as the khanate developed closer ties to Islamic culture.

The Rise and Transformation of the Chagatai Khanate and Its Legacy in Central Asia

Chagatai Khanate around 1300 AD. Author: Thomas A. Lessman. Source URL: https://www.worldhistorymaps.info

The Chagatai Khanate encompassed a diverse population, including Turkic, Uyghur, Sogdian, and Persian peoples. While Uyghurs held privileged positions in the administration due to their literacy, tensions simmered over religious and cultural differences. Many Uyghurs remained Buddhist or Manichaean, while other Turkic tribes in the khanate practiced Tengriism or Islam. ^250

• • •• • • ••• •• •• • ••• •• • •• •••• •• • •• • • • • • ••• • • • •• ••• • • •• •
• •• • •• •• • • • • • •• •

In the mid-14th century, the Chagatai Khanate was weakened by fragmentation until Tughluk Timur (1329–1363 CE) sought to reunify it. Tughluk Timur, seven generations removed from Chagatai Khan, was born into challenging circumstances following the death of his father, Isan Bugha Khan, which left the Moghul succession in disarray. With the support of influential allies like Amir Bulaji, Tughluk Timur was declared Khan in Aksu, marking the beginning of his reign. This period of revival under Tughluk Timur is well-documented in both the *Tarikh-i-Rashidi* by Mirza Muhammad Haidar Dughlat and modern historical analyses, including Michal Biran's *The Empire of the Chagatai Khanate*. ^254

Upon his rise in 1353, Tughluk Timur converted to Islam. His conversion to Islam is one of the most pivotal moments in the history of the Eastern Chagatai Khanate (Moghulistan), leading to the widespread Islamization of the Mongol tribes in the region. Tughluk Timur's personal conversion set the stage for the mass Islamization of

94

Moghulistan. It is said that under his rule, approximately 160,000 Mongols converted to Islam, reflecting both voluntary conversions and those enacted through state-supported religious campaigns. According to Mirza Haidar, Tughluk Timur mandated Islam as the state religion, which encouraged many Mongol tribes to adopt the faith, blending it with their nomadic traditions. Moghulistan, which had been a stronghold of Mongol shamanism and Buddhism, became a center of Islamic culture and practice. The process was further cemented by subsequent rulers of Moghulistan, who upheld Islam as the foundation of their political legitimacy and cultural identity.

According to the *Tarikh-i-Rashidi* by Mirza Muhammad Haidar Dughlat, Tughluk Timur proclaimed:

"The faith of Islam is like a light that illuminates the darkness. I will bring the light of Islam to this land." [251]

During Tughluk Timur's reign, Almaliq, around the modern Uyghur city of Ghulja, served as his capital and the center of his efforts to unify the Chagatai Khanate. It was in this city that Sheikh Jamal al-Din reportedly influenced Tughluk Timur's conversion to Islam, a turning point that led to the mass Islamization of Moghulistan. Almaliq's strategic and cultural importance made it an ideal base for Tughluk Timur to consolidate his authority and propagate his religious and political reforms.

Under the reign of Tughluk Timur (1347–1363), the Mongols began to embrace Islam, a shift that marked the start of their integration into the Turkic-Islamic cultural sphere. This transformation was not immediate but evolved over generations. By adopting the Turkic language, Islamic faith, and sedentary agricultural and urban practices, the Mongols gradually became Turkicized, blending their nomadic heritage with the customs and traditions of the Turkic peoples they ruled alongside.

The tomb of Tughluk Timur Khan located in Korgas, near Gulja. Photo credit: Daniel C. Waugh.

Tughluk Timur's son Khizr Khoja, born around 1363 in Moghulistan, served as Khan of Moghulistan from 1389 to 1399, during which he played a pivotal role in the further Islamization of the region. Building on his father's efforts, he sought to unify the Chagatai Khanate under Islam, targeting Buddhist Qocho for integration. Khizr Khoja's military campaign was decisive, and by 1393, the Chagatai forces had successfully captured Qocho (Turpan). This conquest effectively ended the Uyghur Qocho Kingdom, dismantling its independent rule and absorbing it into the Chagatai Khanate. The economic and religious motivations were clear: unifying the region under Islam would strengthen the Khanate and eliminate religious divides. ^252

Khizr Khoja's conquest marked the beginning of the total Islamization of the Uyghur population in the Tarim Basin. As Islamic institutions replaced Buddhist temples, Uyghur

96

society increasingly embraced Islam, integrating the region more closely with the Chagatai Khanate's religious identity. This shift transformed the social and cultural landscape, deeply influencing Uyghur history. ^253

• • •• • • •• •• • ••• •• • • • • • • • ••• • • ••• • •• ••• • •• •• • • • • • • •• ••• • •
• •••• • •• • • • • ••• • • • •• ••• • • • • • • • • • • •• •

The relationship between Timur, also known as Amir Timur, Tamerlane or Timur the Lame, and the Eastern Chagatai Khanate began when Tughluk Timur launched a campaign into Transoxiana in the early 1360s. Tughluk Timur sought to unify key cities such as Samarkand, Bukhara, and Shahrisabz, which were fragmented under competing factions at the time. The Barlas clan, to which Timur belonged, was one of the key players in this fragmented landscape. Tughluk Timur's campaign forced Hajji Beg, the leader of the Barlas, to flee, creating a leadership vacuum. Timur, recognizing the futility of resistance against the superior forces of Tughluk Timur, chose to submit. This pragmatic decision allowed him to secure a subordinate position within Tughluk Timur's framework of rule.

Tughluk Timur's policy of nominally integrating Transoxiana, which was part of the Western Chagatai Khanate at the time, into his domain brought temporary stability to the region but also demonstrated to Timur the vulnerabilities of Moghulistan's rule. The Eastern Chagatai Khanate, while powerful, was plagued by tribal divisions and its reliance on nomadic governance, which limited its ability to control more urbanized regions like Transoxiana effectively.

The Timurid Empire, founded by Timur in 1370, posed a formidable threat to the Chagatai Khanate. Timur sought legitimacy by conquering former Mongol khanates and unleashed devastating campaigns across Transoxiana and the Tarim Basin. By 1378, Timur captured the Chagatai capital of Almaliq, bringing the Chagatai Khanate under his control. His conquests included the sacking of cities like Kashgar and Balasaghun.

In 1405, the Chagatai Khanate fragmented significantly following Timur's death, which destabilized Central Asia and disrupted any remaining Chagatai authority. This division resulted in the Chagatai Khanate splitting into two main regions: Moghulistan in the east, governed by Chagatai descendants and local leaders like the Dughlat Emirs, and the Western Chagatai Khanate, or Transoxiana, which fell under the control of Timur's successors. ^254

The Dughlat Emirs, Mongol aristocrats from the Barlas clan, wielded significant power in the eastern Chagatai Khanate. Though nominally under Chagatai authority, they ruled Kashgar, Yarkent, Khotan, and Aksu with de facto independence, maintaining these cities as trade and cultural centers. Supporting poets and scholars, they fostered a unique blend of Uyghur and Islamic heritage, bridging Buddhist and Muslim influences in the region. ^255

The Chaghatay language, deeply rooted in the Uyghur linguistic tradition, represents one of the most significant cultural and intellectual achievements of the medieval Turkic world. Emerging as the dominant literary and administrative language of Central Asia during the Chaghatay Khanate, it served as a critical medium for preserving and advancing the Uyghurs' cultural heritage. The Uyghurs, whose linguistic and literary contributions shaped the very foundation of Chaghatay, played a central role in its development and widespread use. ^250

Chaghatay became a unifying language for the diverse Turkic-speaking peoples of Central Asia, transcending regional dialects and establishing a shared medium of communication, governance, and artistic expression. While its vocabulary and syntax were influenced by Persian and Arabic, its core remained distinctly Turkic, drawing heavily from the Uyghur language. This linguistic continuity highlighted the Uyghurs' historical significance as cultural leaders, whose intellectual and artistic contributions provided a foundation for broader Turkic identity. ^249

The influence of Chaghatay extended far beyond the borders of the Chaghatay Khanate. It became the lingua franca for much of Central Asia, used not only by the Uyghurs but also by other Turkic-speaking peoples, including the Timurids and the early Mughals in South Asia. Its widespread use in governance, literature, and cultural exchange solidified its role as one of the most influential languages of the medieval Turkic world. ^252

The Chaghatay period witnessed a remarkable flourishing of literature, philosophy, and historiography, with Uyghur scholars and poets playing pivotal roles. One of the most renowned figures of this era was Ali-Shir Nava'i, who elevated Chaghatay to a sophisticated literary language capable of rivaling Persian. Nava'i's works, including his lyrical poetry and treatises on language and philosophy, celebrated the richness of Turkic expression while reinforcing the Uyghurs' contributions to Central Asian culture. ^253

An exquisite page from *Maḥbūb al-Qulūb* by Alisher Nava'i, showcasing intricate calligraphy and timeless artistry. Credit: Library of Congress.

Chaghatay also became a vehicle for the preservation and dissemination of Uyghur identity and traditions. By integrating Islamic values with Uyghur customs, the literature of this period showcased a synthesis of spiritual and cultural elements that resonated deeply with the Turkic-speaking world. Historical records, moral treatises, and artistic expressions produced in Chaghatay not only celebrated Uyghur achievements but also ensured their enduring legacy within the broader Islamic and Turkic civilizations. ^251

The cultural and intellectual achievements of the Chaghatay era, rooted in Uyghur traditions, left an indelible mark on the history of Central Asia. The language's literary sophistication and adaptability enabled it to endure as a cornerstone of Turkic literature well into the modern period. For the Uyghurs, Chaghatay represents not just a linguistic milestone but also a testament to their historical role as innovators and preservers of Central Asian culture. ^254

• • •• •• • • • • •

The Mongol invasions, the establishment of the Chagatai Khanate, and the rise of the Timurid and Yarkent Khanates were transformative in Central Asian history. While the

Uyghur Qocho Kingdom initially preserved its autonomy by submitting to Genghis Khan, it ultimately integrated into the larger Mongol and Timurid empires. Although the Karakhanid Khaganate was dismantled by Mongol conquest, Uyghur influence endured, culminating in the Yarkent Khanate. This Khanate symbolized Uyghur adaptability and cultural endurance within the evolving political landscape of Central Asia, marking the Uyghurs' lasting legacy in the region. ^256

Notes

248. Morgan, David. *The Mongols*. Cambridge: Blackwell, 1991, 50–52.
249. Biran, Michal. *The Empire of the Chagatai Khanate*. Leiden: Brill, 2005, 80–82.
250. Golden, Peter B. *An Introduction to the History of the Turkic Peoples*. Wiesbaden: Otto Harrassowitz, 1992, 214–217.
251. Dughlat, Mirza Muhammad Haidar. *Tarikh-i-Rashidi*. 16th century.
252. Morgan, David. *The Mongols*. Cambridge: Blackwell, 1991, 100–102.
253. Golden, Peter B. *An Introduction to the History of the Turkic Peoples*. Wiesbaden: Otto Harrassowitz, 1992, 246–248.
254. Biran, Michal. *The Empire of the Chagatai Khanate*. Leiden: Brill, 2005, 80–82.
255. Dughlat, Mirza Muhammad Haidar. *Tarikh-i-Rashidi*. 16th century.
256. Morgan, David. *The Mongols*. Cambridge: Blackwell, 1991, 150–152.

The Yarkent Khaganate, established in 1514 by Sultan Said Khan, spanned until 1705 and was recognized by several names, each reflecting its cultural and dynastic heritage. Locally, it was referred to as the Saidiyya Khanate, honoring Sultan Said Khan's founding lineage. The khanate was also called the Altishahr Khanate ("Khanate of the Six Cities"), referring to key cities in the Tarim Basin. In Arabic, it was named Khānīyat Yārkand or Khānīyat Saʿīdiyya, and in Persian as Khānāt-e Yārkand or Dawlat-e Saʿīdiyya, showing the influence of its multiethnic composition. ^257

The Yarkent Khaganate emerged in the early 16th century amidst the political disarray that followed the decline of the Timurid Empire. East Turkistan, fragmented by internal conflicts and a lack of centralized governance, presented an opportunity for dynamic leadership. In 1514, Sultan Said Khan, a descendant of the illustrious Chagatai lineage, capitalized on this power vacuum to establish the Yarkent Khaganate. Declaring Yarkent as its capital, he positioned the khanate strategically along the Silk Road, transforming it into a hub for trade, cultural exchange, and regional influence. ^258

Sultan Said Khan sought not just territorial control but a deeper unity within the region, integrating Islamic governance with Uyghur traditions to create a stable framework. His leadership was welcomed by local communities, who viewed his reign as a revival of Uyghur self-rule after centuries of external domination and internal strife. ^259

The Yarkent Khaganate: A Legacy of Power, Culture, and Diplomacy, and the Tragedy of Disunity

· · ·· · · · · · · ··· · ··· · ·· · · ·· · ···· · ··· ·

To unify East Turkistan, Sultan Said Khan overcame significant challenges, including rival factions and entrenched leaders. One of his most notable victories came in 1514, when he defeated Mirza Aba Bakr Dughlat, a ruler known for his oppressive governance of Yarkent, Kashgar, and Khotan. Said Khan's victory consolidated territories stretching from Kashgar to Kumul and declared the Yarkent Khaganate. In addition to his military triumphs, Sultan Said Khan achieved significant diplomatic victories. He maintained strong relations with his cousin Babur, the founder of the Indian Mughal Empire, and established a cooperative alliance with the empire. This relationship facilitated cultural and economic exchanges between East Turkistan and Northern India, further bolstering the Yarkent Khaganate's prominence in the region. ^260

The khanate's influence extended beyond the Tarim Basin, incorporating regions such as the Northern Tengri-Tagh area, the Ili Valley, and and nearby areas. These territories, vital for their strategic and economic significance, served as buffer zones and trade conduits. The inclusion of these regions significantly enhanced the khanate's access to Silk Road networks and expanded its geopolitical influence across Central Asia.

By consolidating these lands, Sultan Said Khan not only unified fragmented regions but also secured a legacy of Uyghur sovereignty within a larger Islamic governance framework.

· · ·· · ····· ·· ·· · · ·· · · ·· · · · · ·· ··· ·· ·· · ·

Sultan Said Khan extended the influence of the Yarkent Khaganate through military campaigns aimed at strengthening borders and unifying neighboring communities. However, his ambitions eventually led him toward Tibet, a region embroiled in religious and political turmoil. In 1533, during a campaign in the harsh Himalayan terrain, logistical challenges and disease devastated his forces, ultimately leading to his death. ^262

At its height, the Yarkent Khaganate's territories encompassed a vast region, including modern-day East Turkistan, Kyrgyzstan, southeastern Kazakhstan, Uzbekistan, parts of Southwest Central Asia, and Kashmir. Its core cities included Yarkent, Kashgar, Aksu, Khotan, Turpan, and Kumul. Regions like the Ili Valley and Kashmir served as both trade hubs and strategic buffer zones, reinforcing the khanate's political and economic strength. ^263

Following Sultan Said Khan, Sultan Abdurashid Khan (r. 1533–1565) maintained the stability of the khanate and presided over a period of cultural flourishing. His contributions to Islamic scholarship and cultural preservation were significant. His successor, Sultan Abdul Karim Khan (r. 1565–1591), struggled with internal divisions but managed to sustain the khanate's economic relevance.

Subsequent rulers faced growing challenges, particularly from external forces. Notably, Sultan Shudja ad-Din Ahmad Khan (r. 1591–1611) attempted to mitigate conflicts among the Naqshbandi Khojas, but his reign was marked by declining centralized authority. Sultan Muhammad Khan (r. 1611–1635) worked to revive economic ties along the Silk Road but faced increasing pressure from the Dzungars, a Mongolic confederation that would eventually play a pivotal role in the khanate's decline.

• • •• • • ••• •• ••• •• • ••• • •• • •• • • ••• • •• • •• • • •• • ••• •

Under Sultan Said Khan and his successor Sultan Abdurashid Khan (r. 1533–1565), the Yarkent Khaganate experienced a golden age of cultural and intellectual flourishing. This period saw the establishment of madrasas (Islamic schools) that attracted scholars from across Central Asia, while cities like Kashgar emerged as renowned centers of literature, poetry, and Islamic scholarship. ^264

One of the most celebrated cultural achievements was the compilation of the Twelve Muqams by Amannisa Khan, wife of Sultan Abdurashid Khan. This collection of Uyghur musical compositions, blending Persian, Turkic, and local influences, became a cornerstone of Uyghur culture. Amannisa Khan's contributions reflect the khanate's emphasis on preserving and promoting cultural heritage alongside Islamic values. ^265

• • •• • • • •• • • ••• • •• •••• • •• • • • • •• • ••• • • • • • • •• • • • ••• • •• •• • •• ••• • •
• • • •• •

The later rulers of the Yarkent Khaganate faced growing internal and external pressures. They sought to maintain stability, but divisions among the Naqshbandi Khojas, particularly between the Aq Taghliks (White Mountain) and Qara Taghliks (Black Mountain) factions, weakened central authority. ^266

By the mid-17th century, these internal divisions allowed external forces like the Dzungar Mongols to intervene. In 1678, Dzungar leader Galdan Boshugtu Khan supported Afaq Khoja's faction, further eroding the khanate's autonomy. Afaq Khoja, with Dzungar backing, eventually established a theocratic state, increasing taxation and religious oversight, which fueled local unrest. This marked the beginning of the end for the Yarkent Khaganate, which continued under Dzungar influence until the Qing annexation of the region in 1759. ^267

The Yarkent Khaganate: A Legacy of Power, Culture, and Diplomacy, and the Tragedy of Disunity

The Yarkent Khaganate's strategic location along the Silk Road made it a key player in transcontinental trade, facilitating the exchange of goods, ideas, and cultural practices between East Asia, Persia, and the Indian subcontinent. Cities like Yarkent and Kashgar became bustling trade hubs, attracting merchants, artisans, and scholars from across Eurasia. ^268

Architecturally, the khanate left a lasting legacy. Grand mosques, palaces, and caravanserais built during this period exemplify a blend of Islamic, Persian, and Central Asian influences. Notable structures, such as the Tomb of Sultan Said Khan, remain as testaments to the region's wealth, cultural refinement, and commitment to Islamic principles.

The Yarkent Khaganate, lasting from 1514 to 1705, left a rich cultural, religious, and architectural legacy that continues to shape modern Uyghur identity. As a symbol of Uyghur and Turkic heritage, the khanate represents a period of autonomy, Islamic unity, and cultural prosperity. This legacy is celebrated among Uyghurs today, embodying a sense of shared identity and historical pride. ^269

The khanate's role as a Silk Road hub facilitated not only economic exchanges but also cultural and intellectual advancements that endure in Uyghur traditions. Its emphasis on arts, such as the Twelve Muqams, and its contributions to Islamic scholarship established a foundation for Uyghur cultural identity. Architecturally, its grand mosques and palaces continue to inspire admiration and serve as historical landmarks.

Religiously, the Yarkent Khaganate's embrace of Islam and its integration with Naqshbandi Sufi traditions reinforced the spiritual fabric of the Uyghur people. The legacy of leaders like Sultan Said Khan and Sultan Abdurashid Khan exemplifies governance rooted in justice, inclusivity, and economic prosperity. The Yarkent Khaganate remains a testament to Uyghur resilience, creativity, and cultural sophistication. ^270

Notes

257.   Bregel, Yuri. *An Historical Atlas of Central Asia*. Leiden: Brill, 2003.
258.   Kim, Hodong. *The History of the Yarkand Khanate*. Cambridge: Cambridge University Press, 2014.
259.   Dughlat, Mirza Muhammad Haidar. *Tarikh-i-Rashidi*. 16th century.
260.   Bregel, Yuri. *An Historical Atlas of Central Asia*. Leiden: Brill, 2003.

261. Kim, Hodong. *The History of the Yarkand Khanate*. Cambridge: Cambridge University Press, 2014, 48–50.
262. Bregel, Yuri. *An Historical Atlas of Central Asia*. Leiden: Brill, 2003.
263. Kim, Hodong. *The History of the Yarkand Khanate*. Cambridge: Cambridge University Press, 2014.
264. Dughlat, Mirza Muhammad Haidar. *Tarikh-i-Rashidi*. 16th century.
265. Dughlat, Mirza Muhammad Haidar. *Tarikh-i-Rashidi*. 16th century.
266. Kim, Hodong. *The History of the Yarkand Khanate*. Cambridge: Cambridge University Press, 2014.
267. Bregel, Yuri. *An Historical Atlas of Central Asia*. Leiden: Brill, 2003.
268. Kim, Hodong. *The History of the Yarkand Khanate*. Cambridge: Cambridge University Press, 2014.
269. Bregel, Yuri. *An Historical Atlas of Central Asia*. Leiden: Brill, 2003.
270. Kim, Hodong. *The History of the Yarkand Khanate*. Cambridge: Cambridge University Press, 2014.

Sultan Said Khan: The Architect of a Unified Turkistan

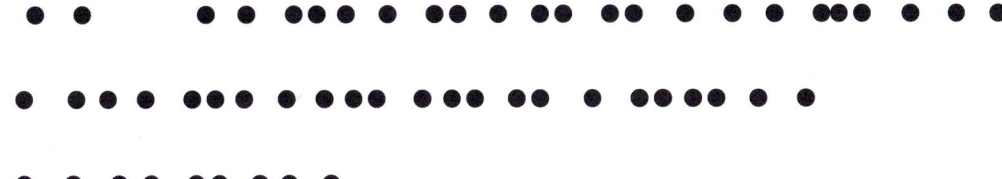

Sultan Said Khan's story is primarily chronicled in *Tarikh-i-Rashidi* by Mirza Muhammad Haidar Dughlat, who was both a historian and a key figure in the events surrounding the Sultan's rise to power.[271] Sultan Said Khan, born in the late 15th century, was the ruler of the Yarkent Khanate, a Turkic-Moghul state in Central Asia. He played a pivotal role in unifying Turkistan and expanding the influence of Islam in the region.[272]

Sultan Said Khan was a scion of the Chagatai Khanate and deeply influenced by his upbringing in a time of political fragmentation. His youth coincided with the decline of the Moghulistan Khanate, and he grew up amidst the ambitions of rival Turkic and Mongol factions.[273] As Dughlat notes, his early years were spent observing the political maneuvers of his father, Sultan Ahmad Alaq, and this honed his understanding of governance and warfare.[271] The broader context of political instability in Central Asia during this time has also been explored in *The Silk Roads and Beyond* by Daniel C. Waugh.[276]

The pivotal moment in the conquest of Turkistan came with the siege of Yarkent, then a prosperous and fortified city. Said Khan's forces faced fierce resistance, but his tactical genius proved insurmountable. Under his command, engineers deployed sappers to weaken the city walls. Addressing his troops before the final assault, he stated:

"Brothers, the strength of a fortress lies not in its walls but in the will of its defenders. Break their will, and the walls shall fall."[271]

The city eventually capitulated, marking a significant milestone in his campaign. Said Khan, true to his principles, prohibited wanton looting, ordering instead:

"Let the people of Yarkent see the justice of their new ruler. Take only what is necessary for our soldiers; leave the rest to rebuild."[271]

The *History of India as Told by Its Own Historians* provides corroborating accounts of Sultan Said Khan's policies toward the conquered cities, emphasizing his preference for justice and rebuilding over plunder.^277

With Yarkent secured, Said Khan turned his attention to Kashgar and Yangi Hisar. These cities, though formidable in defense, lacked coordinated leadership, allowing his forces to claim victory with minimal bloodshed. After entering Kashgar, he performed a symbolic act of prayer at the shrine of Satuk Bughra Khan, the first Muslim Turkic ruler, proclaiming:

"As Satuk embraced the faith to unite his people, so shall we bring unity to Turkistan under the banner of justice and Islam."^271

After the conquest of major cities like Yarkent, Kashgar, and Yangi Hisar, his influence extended eastward to regions like Turpan and Kumul, solidifying his control over the broader region. While addressing his court following the successful conquest of these territories, Sultan Said Khan is recorded to have remarked:

"From the bustling bazaars of Kashgar to the serene oases of Turpan and Kumul, let the lands of Turkistan stand united. These are not just conquests of land but victories of justice and faith. Let each city flourish under our banner, for their prosperity is our legacy."^271

Sultan Said Khan was not only a warrior but also a statesman. Following his military victories, he employed diplomacy to secure alliances with local community leaders and ensure the loyalty of the populace. He appointed capable administrators from among his relatives and trusted advisors, declaring:

"A ruler cannot stand alone; he is but the shadow of his people. Choose wisely, for their strength shall be our foundation."^271

His governance style has been extensively analyzed by modern historians, including Timothy Stewart, who highlights the integration of Turkic, Islamic, and Mongol traditions in administration.^278

His reforms included measures to improve trade routes, protect caravans, and encourage scholarship and religious study, cementing his legacy as a just ruler.^273 His patronage of

Islamic scholars and support for madrasas established his reputation as a builder of both spiritual and material prosperity.^274

• • •• • • ••• • •• • • •• • • •• ••• ••

In his later years, Sultan Said Khan reflected on the nature of power and conquest, particularly after a series of spiritual experiences. He remarked:

"Victory in battle is fleeting, but the establishment of justice endures. The sword may win a kingdom, but it is the pen that sustains it."^271

"Turkistan is a land of diverse peoples and beliefs. Let no ruler imagine it can be held by force alone. The hearts of the people are the true citadel."^271

• • •• • • • • • •

The tomb of Sultan Said Khan located in Yarkent. Image credit: FileUpload Bot (Colegota), licensed under CC BY-SA 4.0. Source: Wikimedia Commons

Sultan Said Khan's death marked the end of an era, but his legacy endured in the Yarkent Khanate, which remained a significant power in Central Asia for close to two centuries.

His ability to unite Turkistan under a single banner and to rule with justice and wisdom is a testament to his vision as both a conqueror and a statesman.^275

Notes

271. Mirza Muhammad Haidar Dughlat, *Tarikh-i-Rashidi* (The History of Rashid).
272. Golden, Peter B. *Central Asia in World History*. Oxford: Oxford University Press, 2011.
273. Bosworth, Clifford Edmund. *The New Islamic Dynasties: A Chronological and Genealogical Manual*. Edinburgh: Edinburgh University Press, 1996.
274. Bregel, Yuri. *An Historical Atlas of Central Asia*. Leiden: Brill, 2003.
275. Hodgson, Marshall G. S. *The Venture of Islam: Conscience and History in a World Civilization, Volume 2*. Chicago: University of Chicago Press, 1974.
276. Waugh, Daniel C. *The Silk Roads and Beyond*. Seattle: University of Washington, 2004.
277. Elliot, H. M., and John Dowson. *The History of India as Told by Its Own Historians*. London: Trübner & Co., 1867.
278. Stewart, Timothy. *The Khans of Eastern Turkistan and Their Reign*. Historical Perspectives Journal 12, no. 3 (2018): 45–67.

Afaq Khoja: The Leader Who Opened the Gates to Foreign Influence in East Turkistan

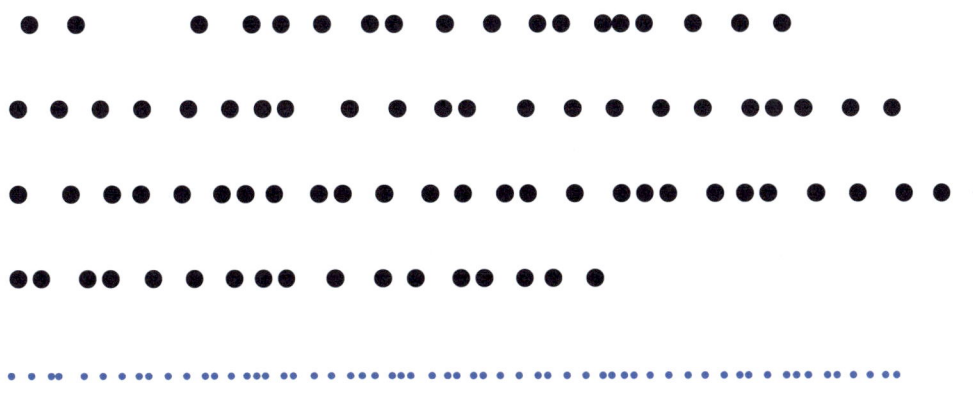

The Khojas trace their origins to Makhdum-i A'zam (Ahmad Kasani, 1461–1542), a revered Naqshbandi Sufi sheikh from Samarkand. Known as "The Great Master," Makhdum-i A'zam was esteemed as a descendant of the Prophet Muhammad and was influential in Central Asia during the 15th and 16th centuries.^279 His teachings, centered on Islamic ethics, meditation (zikr), and strict adherence to Sunni principles, gained significant influence in the major Islamic centers of Bukhara and Samarkand. His followers, known as the Khojas ("masters" or "learned men"), were respected as spiritual and eventually political leaders.^280

In the mid-16th century, the Khojas began expanding eastward into East Turkistan. This movement was led by Makhdum-i A'zam's grandson, Khoja Muhammad Yusuf, who extended the Naqshbandi order's influence to the Turkic Muslim populations of the Tarim Basin.^281 The shared Islamic faith and cultural ties between the Khojas and the Turkic-speaking communities facilitated their entry, allowing the Khojas to establish authority in cities like Kashgar and Yarkent and gradually compete for political power in the region.^282

Afaq Khoja (1626–1694), also known as Khoja Afaq, was a charismatic Naqshbandi Sufi leader born in Kumul. As the son of Muhammad Yusuf Khoja, Afaq Khoja leveraged his family's Naqshbandi legacy to consolidate religious and political influence in Eas Turkistan. ^283 Building on the groundwork laid by his forebears, he became a significant figure in cities like Kashgar and Yarkent, where he skillfully combined his spiritual leadership with political authority, solidifying the Khoja family's prominence in the region.^284

As a Naqshbandi Sufi leader, he commanded deep respect among the Muslim population for his piety and his role as a spiritual guide. His reputation as a miracle worker and a healer enhanced his status as a religious figure, and he used this influence to build a strong political base in East Turkistan. ^285 Afaq Khoja earned a reputation as a Sufi master, attracting followers among Uyghur and Turkic Muslim communities. His teachings and reputed miracles garnered substantial support, empowering him to challenge the local Yarkent Khanate. His influence put him at odds with Isma'il Khan, ruler of the Yarkent Khanate, who saw Afaq Khoja as a political threat.^286

• • •• • • ••• ••• ••• • •• • •• ••• • • • •• •• • • • •••• • •• •• • • • ••• ••• ••••• •

As his power grew, Isma'il Khan exiled Afaq Khoja, forcing him to seek refuge. During his exile, Afaq Khoja traveled to regions like Kashmir and Tibet, where he received temporary shelter from the Dalai Lama's court.^287 This period strengthened his resolve to reclaim his influence in East Turkistan and made him recognize the necessity of military support to achieve his goals, despite the religious implications of collaborating with non-Muslim allies.^288.

• • •• • ••••• • • •• ••• ••• • •• • •• • • ••• •• •• •• •• ••• •• • • ••

In a strategic move, Afaq Khoja allied with the Qalmaqs, a Mongol group known for their military might, despite his reservations about working with non-Muslims.^289 The Qalmaq törä (tribal leader) supported his campaign, and their combined forces launched an attack on Sultan Isma'il Khan's domain. This alliance led to Afaq Khoja's successful campaign in Kashgar and Yarkent in 1678, marking the beginning of a period when he established himself as a ruler under the support of Dzungar military backing, and he also appointed his son, Khoja Yahya (Khan Khoja), as governor of Kashgar. Realizing further resistance was futile, Sultan Isma'il Khan negotiated a surrender, securing local autonomy while restricting Qalmaq interference in religious matters.^290.

• •• • ••••• • •• ••••• • • • • • ••• • •• •• •• •• •• • • ••

As Afaq Khoja, leader of the Aq Taghlik faction, sought to consolidate his authority under Dzungar suzerainty, he strategically used marriage alliances to strengthen his political influence.^291 Afaq Khoja married Khanum Padshah, also known as Padshah Begum, the sister of Muhammad Amin Khan, ruler of Turpan and brother of Sultan Isma'il Khan. A prominent figure in the Chagatai lineage, Padshah Begum's marriage to

Afaq Khoja was a calculated political union that forged a powerful bond with the ruling elite of the Yarkent Khanate.^292

Padshah Begum was not only a royal consort but also a politically astute figure whose influence extended beyond her marital alliance. Her position as Padshah Begum symbolized the merging of spiritual and political authority, with her support solidifying Afaq Khoja's claim to power. Leveraging this alliance, Afaq Khoja temporarily reinstated his brother-in-law, Muḥammad Amin Khan, as Sultan, balancing his spiritual leadership with governance demands.^293 However, Muḥammad Amin Khan's attempts to stabilize the fractured khanate faced resistance from rival factions, exacerbating internal strife.^294

• • •• • • • • •• •••• ••• • ḥ• • • • • •• •• • •• •• • ••

During his reign, Muḥammad Amin Khan launched a significant raid against the Qalmaqs and their Dzungar allies, capturing many qalmaqs including several high-ranking töräs, with Afaq Khoja's tacit approval.^294 This bold move temporarily bolstered his authority and weakened Dzungar influence in the region. Despite this success, internal tensions persisted. In 1694, Muḥammad Amin Khan was betrayed by a retainer and killed, marking the end of independent Uyghur leadership in East Turkistan.^295

Following his death, the Dzungar Khanate**,** under the leadership of Ghaldan Boshugtu Khan, solidified control over the region by installing puppet rulers. They appointed figurehead khans to maintain nominal control while real power was exercised by Dzungar authorities and their local allies.^296 The Yarkent Khanate was effectively relegated to a vassal state under Dzungar domination. Afaq Khoja died later that year in 1694 and was buried in the Afaq Khoja Mausoleum near Kashgar, which remains a significant cultural and historical site in the region.^297

• • •• • ••• •• • •• •• •• • •• ••• • •• ••• •• •• •••• • • •

Although Afaq Khoja achieved military success with Qalmaq support, he reportedly came to deeply regret this alliance, feeling it had compromised his spiritual integrity. Reflecting on his actions, he lamented:

"On the day I took these kingdoms with the support of the Qalmaq army and occupied the throne of the sultanate, in my embarrassment and shame, I felt I would never be able to raise my head before God and the Apostle."^298

In his later years, Afaq Khoja turned increasingly to Sufi practices, seeking atonement for what he saw as a profound compromise of his spiritual values.

The regret of Afaq Khoja: "I felt I would never be able to raise my head before God and the Apostle"

• • • • • • • • •• ••• •• ••• •• •• • •• •• •• •

As a leader, Afaq Khoja struggled to reconcile his spiritual ideals with the political realities of governance. He continued to lead Sufi meditation (zikr) circles and guide his followers, yet governance often clashed with his principles. This tension was evident when he tacitly approved a raid against the Qalmaqs led by Muḥammad Emin Khan, which resulted in the capture of thousands of Qalmaq soldiers.^299

Afaq Khoja: The Leader Who Opened the Gates to Foreign Influence in East Turkistan

Afaq Khoja remained highly respected as a Sufi leader, with his followers admiring his piety and reputed healing abilities. However, his reliance on foreign powers like the Qalmaqs and later the Dzungars undermined Uyghur sovereignty.^300 His reign marked the beginning of foreign influence in the region, as internal divisions weakened local defenses.^301.

The consequences of Afaq Khoja's alliances reverberated long after his death. By inviting foreign powers like the Dzungars into the region, Afaq Khoja inadvertently paved the way for increased external control, not only disrupting Uyghur sovereignty but also setting the stage for subsequent interventions by larger empires, including the Qing Empire.^302 The growing dominance of the Dzungars further destabilized East Turkistan, as local leaders became increasingly reliant on foreign powers to maintain their positions, deepening political fragmentation.^303

The rivalry between the Aq Taghlik and Qara Taghlik factions within the Khoja family, exacerbated by Dzungar manipulation, created enduring divisions among the Uyghur population.^304 These divisions eroded the cohesion necessary for a unified Uyghur resistance against foreign domination, allowing the Dzungars to consolidate their influence. The subsequent Qing conquest in 1759 capitalized on this weakened political structure, marking the beginning of a long period of external control over East Turkistan.^305

While Afaq Khoja's spiritual contributions as a Naqshbandi Sufi leader are celebrated, his political decisions remain a subject of intense debate. Supporters argue that his alliances were pragmatic measures to counter immediate threats and consolidate power in a tumultuous era.^306 Critics, however, contend that his actions prioritized short-term gains over long-term independence, ultimately diminishing Uyghur autonomy and accelerating the region's subjugation by external powers.^307

Afaq Khoja's mausoleum near Kashgar, now a significant cultural and historical site, symbolizes the duality of his legacy. For many, it serves as a reminder of his spiritual leadership and the resilience of Uyghur culture. For others, it stands as a cautionary tale of the political compromises that led to the erosion of Uyghur sovereignty.^309

Notes

279. Makhdum-i A'zam, *Tazkirah-i-Azizan*.
280. Bregel, Yuri. *An Historical Atlas of Central Asia*. Leiden: Brill, 2003.
281. Golden, Peter B. *Central Asia in World History*. Oxford: Oxford University Press, 2011.
282. Stewart, Timothy. *The Khans of Eastern Turkistan and Their Reign*. Historical Perspectives Journal 12, no. 3 (2018): 45–67.
283. Kim, Hodong. *The History of the Yarkand Khanate*. Cambridge: Cambridge University Press, 2014.
284. Muhammad Sadiq Kashghari, *Tazkirah-i-Azizan*.
285. Millward, James A. *Eurasian Crossroads: A History of Xinjiang*. Columbia University Press, 2007.
286. Brophy, David. *Uyghur Nation: Reform and Revolution on the Russia-China Frontier*. Harvard University Press, 2016.
287. Waugh, Daniel C. *The Silk Roads and Beyond*. Seattle: University of Washington, 2004.
288. Bregel, Yuri. *An Historical Atlas of Central Asia*. Leiden: Brill, 2003.
289. Muhammad Sadiq Kashghari, *Tazkirah-i-Azizan*.
290. Kim, Hodong. *The History of the Yarkand Khanate*. Cambridge: Cambridge University Press, 2014.
291. Golden, Peter B. *Central Asia in World History*. Oxford: Oxford University Press, 2011.
292. Millward, James A. *Eurasian Crossroads: A History of Xinjiang*. Columbia University Press, 2007.
293. Brophy, David. *Uyghur Nation: Reform and Revolution on the Russia-China Frontier*. Harvard University Press, 2016.
294. Muhammad Sadiq Kashghari, *Tazkirah-i-Azizan*.
295. Golden, Peter B. *Central Asia in World History*. Oxford: Oxford University Press, 2011.
296. Millward, James A. *Eurasian Crossroads: A History of Xinjiang*. Columbia University Press, 2007.
297. Brophy, David. *Uyghur Nation: Reform and Revolution on the Russia-China Frontier*. Harvard University Press, 2016.
298. Muhammad Sadiq Kashghari, *Tazkirah-i-Azizan*.
299. Golden, Peter B. *Central Asia in World History*. Oxford: Oxford University Press, 2011.
300. Brophy, David. *Uyghur Nation: Reform and Revolution on the Russia-China Frontier*. Harvard University Press, 2016.
301. Kim, Hodong. *The History of the Yarkand Khanate*. Cambridge: Cambridge University Press, 2014.
302. Millward, James A. *Eurasian Crossroads: A History of Xinjiang*. Columbia University Press, 2007.
303. Brophy, David. *Uyghur Nation: Reform and Revolution on the Russia-China Frontier*. Harvard University Press, 2016.
304. Muhammad Sadiq Kashghari, *Tazkirah-i-Azizan*.
305. Kim, Hodong. *The History of the Yarkand Khanate*. Cambridge: Cambridge University Press, 2014.
306. Bregel, Yuri. *An Historical Atlas of Central Asia*. Leiden: Brill, 2003.
307. Golden, Peter B. *Central Asia in World History*. Oxford: Oxford University Press, 2011.
308. Waugh, Daniel C. *The Silk Roads and Beyond*. Seattle: University of Washington, 2004.

The Qing Conquest of the East Turkistan: The Fall of the Khoja Rule

In the early 18th century, after the death of Afaq Khoja, his descendants from the Naqshbandi Sufi tradition faced growing conflict with the rival Ishaqi Khoja faction, also known as the Black Mountain Khojas. These internal divisions left Altishahr politically fragmented and increasingly vulnerable to external domination. By 1716, perceiving the Afaqi Khojas as a potential threat to their rule, the Dzungar Khanate exiled the Afaqi family, including Khoja Burhan al-Din, Khoja Jahan, and their relatives, to Ili, to keep them under close surveillance. This strategic exile allowed the Dzungars to keep the Afaqi family under close surveillance while weakening their influence in the Tarim Basin.^309

During this nearly 40-year exile, the Ishaqi Khojas took full advantage of Dzungar patronage to consolidate their power. They acted as intermediaries, managing the Uyghur population of Altishahr on behalf of the Dzungars. By enforcing taxation, suppressing dissent, and ensuring the dominance of their patrons, the Ishaqi Khojas gained significant control. This alliance allowed the Dzungars to maintain stability in the fragmented region while curbing the influence of the exiled Afaqi Khojas.^310

With the Afaqi Khojas sidelined, the Ishaqi Khojas flourished under Dzungar patronage. They leveraged this relationship to suppress rival factions and enforce their rule over Altishahr. However, while the Ishaqi Khojas thrived, their rule brought significant hardship to the Uyghur population. Heavy taxation, forced labor, and exploitation became the hallmarks of Dzungar control, enforced through the Ishaqi Khojas. These oppressive measures fueled widespread resentment among the Uyghurs, who grew increasingly disillusioned with both the Ishaqi leaders and their Dzungar patrons.^311

As discontent spread, the region became a powder keg of unrest, with many Uyghurs longing for liberation from the harsh conditions. This environment of dissatisfaction set

116

the stage for the Qing Empire to intervene. Positioned as an alternative to Dzungar exploitation, the Qing capitalized on Uyghur frustrations to justify their expansion into the region. The reliance of the Black Mountain Khojas on Dzungar support further exposed their fragility, paving the way for external forces to challenge their dominance.^312

• • •• • • • • • • •••• ••• •• • •• • • • •• • ••• •• • • • • •• • •• •• • •

The Qing Empire initially sought to avoid direct governance over territories beyond the Dzungar Khanate. Their strategy centered on maintaining "protective screens outside the borders," relying on vassal states like the Kazakhs and Kyrgyz to act as buffers for Qing-controlled areas.^313 Similarly, in the southern regions of the Tengri Mountains, the Qing sought to stabilize Uyghur society by co-opting local leaders from prominent factions.

Following their decisive defeat of the Dzungars, the Qing encountered Khoja Burhan al-Din and his brother Khoja Jahan of the Afaqi Khojas, who had been exiled to Ili by the Dzungars decades earlier. The Qing recognized the influence of these leaders among the Uyghur population and sought to use them as intermediaries. Khoja Burhan al-Din and Khoja Jahan were granted a carefully crafted opportunity to return to the Tarim Basin under the Qing's auspices. The Qing's plan was twofold: first, to re-establish order in the fractured region through leaders who held religious and social legitimacy, and second, to ensure that these leaders remained beholden to Qing authority.

The Qing carefully vetted the Khojas before reinstating them, emphasizing their allegiance to the empire. Imperial records indicate that the Afaqi Khojas were presented with ceremonial seals of office and were instructed to oversee Uyghur society under strict Qing supervision. This symbolic gesture underscored their subordinate role while appealing to the Uyghur population, who viewed the Khojas as legitimate leaders due to their lineage from Afaq Khoja.^314

Through this approach, the Qing sought to integrate the southern Tengri Mountain regions into their administrative framework without deploying a large-scale occupying force. The Khojas, with their established religious influence and local connections, were seen as an ideal bridge between the Qing rulers and the Uyghur communities. However, the Qing's reliance on these intermediaries was not without risk, as their loyalties remained precarious—a fact that became evident when Khoja Jahan declared independence in 1757, triggering a rebellion that threatened Qing control.

• • •• • • •• •• • • • • •••• ••• • • • • • •• • • •• •• • •• •• • •• ••• •
• • • • • • •• •• • • •• •

In 1755, during their campaign against the Dzungars, the Qing released Afaqi Khoja Burhan al-Din and supported him and his brother Khoja Jahan to govern the south of the

Tengri Mountains as a stabilizing force. However, their return reignited the bitter rivalry between the Afaqi (White Mountain) and Ishaqi (Black Mountain) Khojas. With Qing backing, Burhan al-Din sought to reclaim the throne, while Khoja Jahan, who succeeded Khoja Yusuf after his untimely death from illness, fiercely resisted and dismissed Burhan al-Din as a "*puppet of the Qing.*"^316

The resulting conflict escalated into a full-scale war, with Burhan al-Din strategically targeting key strongholds held by Khoja Jahan. After a series of intense battles, Burhan al-Din ultimately prevailed by employing superior tactics and leveraging his forces' mobility to outmaneuver Khoja Jahan's defenses. After defeating his rival Khoja Jahan in 1756, with Qing assistance, Burhan al-Din attempted to consolidate his rule. Despite Khoja Jahan's determined efforts to rally his military forces and resist, his defeat marked a turning point in the conflict. This prolonged war not only weakened both factions but also provided the Qing with opportunities to tighten their grip on the region. By 1757, Burhan al-Din declared independence from the Qing, framing his rebellion as a defense of Islamic tradition and a bid to restore autonomy.^317

After defeating his rival Khojas, Burhan al-Din drew legitimacy from his lineage as a descendant of Afaq Khoja. In 1757, he declared independence from the Qing. His bold move aimed to establish East Turkistan as a sovereign entity under his leadership.^318

Burhan al-Din's ambition to assert his rule based on his lineage did not gain widespread support among the Uyghurs. His reliance on Qing support and suppression of rival factions eroded his credibility, leaving him isolated and distrusted. Lacking popular support, Burhan al-Din's authority eroded, leaving him increasingly vulnerable.^319 By 1759, Qing forces decisively crushed the Khoja resistance. Fleeing to Badakhshan (modern-day Tajikistan), Burhan al-Din and his brother were betrayed by Sultan Shah of Badakhshan and executed. Their deaths marked the end of significant Uyghur-led political resistance in the Tarim Basin.^320

The collapse of Khoja rule highlighted the perils of internal division and reliance on external alliances. Burhan al-Din's attempts to secure power through Qing support and his subsequent bid for independence alienated key segments of Uyghur society. This loss of unity and trust ultimately led to the downfall of the Afaqi Khojas.^321

The fall of Khoja rule marked a turning point in Uyghur history. The Qing conquest of East Turkistan in 1759 not only ended Uyghur sovereignty but also reshaped the region's political and cultural identity. Although pockets of resistance persisted, the disunity and external dependencies of the Khoja era left East Turkistan under Qing domination for more than a century. The legacy of this era remains a poignant reminder of the challenges and consequences of fragmented leadership in the struggle for independence.^322

Burhan al-Din Khoja led the East Turkistan Army in a significant battle against Qing soldiers near Yashilkul Lake in 1759. Painted 1764 by Jean-Damascène Sallusti.

25.7 The History of the Khojas of East Turkistan

Robert Barkley Shaw (1839–1879)'s *The History of the Khojas of Eastern Turkistan,*^323 , summarized from *Tazkira-i-Azizan ,*^324 , by Muhammad Sadiq Kashghari (born 1725), offers a poignant narrative of the Khoja family's relentless struggle for independence. This account, written in 1785 shortly after the fall of Khoja rule, emphasizes the aspirations, sacrifices, and ultimate fall of the Khojas, providing a Uyghur perspective on their turbulent history.

25.7.1 Ishaqi Khoja Danyal's Unfulfilled Dream (c. 1720s)

Khoja Danyal governed under Qalmaq (Dzungar) domination, paying an annual tribute of 100,000 tangas. Although he maintained stability, he longed for independence. On his deathbed, he entrusted this dream to his sons, declaring:

"I die without attaining the wish of my heart, which is independence from the infidels. May God grant this to my sons."

Despite his ambitions, Danyal could not achieve independence, as the region remained under Dzungar control. His deathbed wish became a driving force for his descendants, shaping their aspirations for freedom in the years that followed.

25.7.2 Khoja Yusuf's Struggles for Independence (1745–1755)

In 1745, the death of Galdan Chiring created instability among the Qalmaqs, providing an opportunity for Khoja Yusuf to act. A visionary leader, he strategically visited the Qalmaq capital at Ili to assess their internal weaknesses and awaited the right moment to rebel.

By 1754, Yusuf fortified Kashgar and allied with the Kipchaks to launch a rebellion. Using subterfuge, he secured permission from the Qalmaqs to return to Kashgar, claiming a false threat from the Kirghiz. Once back, he prepared for war, imprisoning traitors like Khuda Yar, who had conspired against him. Yusuf's leadership reflected his deep understanding of the regional dynamics and his unwavering commitment to liberating his people.

However, Yusuf faced overwhelming opposition from the Qalmaqs and internal betrayal. Illness compounded his struggles, and in 1755, he passed away in Yarkent. His final act was a symbolic ride into the city on horseback, reaffirming his commitment to its people despite his failing health. Yusuf's death marked a turning point, leaving Yarkent vulnerable to external aggression.

25.7.3 The Final War with Rival Khoja Burhan al-Din (1755–1756)

Following Khoja Yusuf's death, his brother Khoja Jahan assumed leadership. He soon faced an invasion by Khoja Burhan al-Din, an Afaqi Khoja aligned with the Qing Empire and supported by Chinese troops and Qalmaq forces. Burhan aimed to seize Kashgar and Yarkent, capitalizing on the power vacuum left by Yusuf's death.

Khoja Jahan rallied Yarkent's defenders, inspiring them with his declaration:

"If he knows himself to be a man, let him learn that others are lions."

Despite initial resistance, internal betrayal weakened Jahan's forces. Ghazi Beg, a trusted commander, orchestrated a deliberate retreat during a critical battle, creating chaos. Yarkent's defenders fled across the frozen Zarafshan River, where many perished in icy waters or fell to pursuing Kirghiz forces allied with Burhan.

Yarkent's fall was a devastating blow to the Khoja faction, marking a significant decline in their ability to resist external domination.

25.7.4 Khoja Abdullah's Last Stand in 1756

Amid the chaos, Khoja Yusuf's son, **Abdullah**, emerged as a symbol of defiance. Refusing to surrender, he declared:

"I would rather die in fight than fall into the hands of these men."

Fleeing with his two children on horseback, Abdullah ensured the survival of the Khoja lineage. Captured Khojas, including Khoja Jahan, were handed over to Burhan-al Din and his Qing allies. Despite promises of clemency, they were executed. As he was led away, Jahan reportedly said:

"Life is only a prison to the faithful, though a paradise to unbelievers."

These words captured the spiritual resilience of the Khojas, even in their darkest hour. Abdullah's courage and determination to preserve his family's legacy left a lasting impression on the narrative of Uyghur resistance.

In *The History of the Khojas of Eastern Turkistan* (edited by N. Elias, 1897), Robert Barkley Shaw provides a detailed account of the region's education system during the late 19th century. Shaw's observations reflect a society where religious instruction was paramount, with primary and advanced education deeply rooted in Islamic traditions.

25.8.1 Primary Education: Maktab Khanas

Primary education in East Turkistan took place in maktab khanas (community schools), often attached to mosques. These schools served as the foundation for both boys and girls. The curriculum focused on reading religious texts and memorizing prayers and Qur'anic verses.

- **Learning Environment**: Students sat in lines, reciting lessons rhythmically in a sing-song tone. To combat the region's bitter cold, children sat in long earthen troughs filled with straw for warmth.
- **Gender Disparity**: Boys progressed to reading and writing Persian and Turki texts, while girls typically received limited education, concluding with basic Qur'anic knowledge taught either at the maktab or at home.

25.8.2 Advanced Education: Madrasas

For students pursuing higher learning, madrasas provided advanced education. These institutions, funded by land and property endowments, were vital centers of Islamic scholarship.

- **Structure and Roles**:
    - The **Akhund** (principal) managed administration and resource allocation.
    - The **Mudarris** (teacher) oversaw instruction.
    - The **Mutawalli** (steward) managed finances and logistics.
    - The **Jarub-Kash** (sweepers) performed menial tasks and maintained facilities.
- **Endowments**: Yarkent alone housed 62 collegiate buildings, with 29 operational madrasas funded by 3,670 patmans of arable land and 198 rental properties, generating 400 yambus of silver annually (about £6,800).

25.8.3 Challenges and Observations

Although the educational system was well-endowed and structured, its effectiveness was limited.

- The emphasis on religious education overshadowed other forms of knowledge.
- Many institutions functioned more as symbols of piety than as active centers of learning.

25.8.4 Conclusion

Robert Barkley Shaw's account highlights the centrality of religion in Uyghur education and underscores inefficiencies within the system. This duality reflects a society striving to preserve its cultural and spiritual heritage while grappling with the limitations of its educational framework.

Notes

309. Millward, James A. *Beyond the Pass: Economy, Ethnicity, and Empire in Qing Central Asia, 1759-1864*. Stanford University Press, 1998, pp. 45–47.
310. Brophy, David. *An Early Manchu Account of the Western Regions*. 2016–2017, pp. 15–16.
311. Perdue, Peter C. *China Marches West: The Qing Conquest of Central Eurasia*. Harvard University Press, 2005, p. 282.
312. Millward, James A. *Beyond the Pass: Economy, Ethnicity, and Empire in Qing Central Asia, 1759-1864*. Stanford University Press, 1998, pp. 62–64.
313. Perdue, Peter C. *China Marches West: The Qing Conquest of Central Eurasia*. Cambridge: Belknap Press of Harvard University Press, 2005.
314. Millward, James A. *Beyond the Pass: Economy, Ethnicity, and Empire in Qing Central Asia, 1759-1864*. Stanford: Stanford University Press, 1998.
315.   Kim, Hodong. *Holy War in China: The Muslim Rebellion and State in Chinese Central Asia, 1864–1877*. Stanford: Stanford University Press, 2004.
316. Brophy, David. *An Early Manchu Account of the Western Regions*. 2016–2017, p. 22.
317. Brophy, David. *An Early Manchu Account of the Western Regions*. 2016–2017, pp. 25–26.
318. Millward, James A. *Eurasian Crossroads: A History of Xinjiang*. Columbia University Press, 2007.
319. Kim, Hodong. *The History of the Yarkand Khanate*. Cambridge University Press, 2004.
320. Perdue, Peter C. *China Marches West: The Qing Conquest of Central Eurasia*. Harvard University Press, 2005, p. 400.
321. Dillon, Michael. *Xinjiang: China's Muslim Far Northwest*. RoutledgeCurzon, 2004.
322. Millward, James A. *Eurasian Crossroads: A History of Xinjiang*. Columbia University Press, 2007.
323. Shaw, R. B., & Elias, N. (Ed.). *The History of the Khojas of Eastern Turkistan: Summarized from the Tazkira-i-Khwajagan of Muhammad Sadiq Kashghari*. Supplement to the *Journal of the Asiatic Society of Bengal*, Vol. LXVI, Part I, 1897.
324. Muhammad Sadiq Kashghari, *Tazkira-i-Azizan*, 1785.

. . ..
.. ..

25.9.1 The The Qing's Self-Perception of Conquest and Domination in Turkistan or "The Eight Cities"

The following original Manchu Qing narrative provides views from the foreign conquerors, reflecting the biased perspectives typical of an invading power seeking to justify their actions. The Qing narrative emphasizes their domination of Turkistan, a foreign Muslim region, through strategic manipulation, military conquest, and moral justification. By incorporating these territories into the Qing Empire, they asserted authority over a culturally and religiously distinct region, presenting themselves as a unifying and civilizing force. The Qing used Burhan al-Din strategically to create internal conflict among Khoja rulers and further divisions among the population, exploiting these fractures to consolidate their control. When Burhan al-Din and his followers ultimately resisted subjugation and rebelled, the Qing military decisively pursued them to Badakhshan and "wiped out" his forces, demonstrating their ruthless suppression of resistance.^325

25.9.1.1 Qing Names of Conquered Muslim Land of Turkistan

The Qing referred to the newly conquered Muslim lands of Turkistan using various terms that reflected their administrative and cultural perception of the region:

1. **"Eight Cities of the Muslims"**
The Qing frequently described the newly conquered territories as the "Eight Cities."^326 The "Eight Cities" referred to by the Qing included the key urban centers of Kashgar, Yarkent, Khotan, Aksu, Kucha, Uchturpan, Turpan, and Korla. This term highlighted the administrative and economic significance of these cities within the region.
2. **"Muslim Territory"**
The Qing described the region as a Muslim land, emphasizing its religious distinction:
"The Muslims are by nature docile and weak... Thus they could not easily resist [the Burut raids]."^327
3. **"Central Nation's New Lands"**
In framing the conquest as part of the Qing Empire's expansion, the text implicitly aligns the territory with the broader concept of Qing sovereignty under the "Central Nation" (China proper).

25.9.2 Summary of Key Excerpts from the Qing Conquest of East Turkistan: Domination of Foreign Muslim Lands

The Qing conquest of Turkistan is portrayed in an early Manchu account as a monumental victory that brought foreign Muslim lands under Qing sovereignty. The narrative emphasizes their role in reshaping these regions through a combination of military might, strategic manipulation of local leaders, and claims of moral authority.

25.9.2.1　　A Historic Conquest of Foreign Lands

The Qing acknowledged that the territory of the Eight Cities (modern-day southern East Turkistan) was a foreign Muslim land, distinct in culture, religion, and governance. Their successful subjugation of this region was framed as an extraordinary accomplishment:

"Having thus pacified the so-called Eight Cities of the Muslims, including Kashgar and Yarkent, the primary task was achieved. As this was an astonishing accomplishment, the like of which has not been seen from ancient times until now..."^328

This victory was celebrated as a significant expansion of Qing rule into a region previously controlled by Muslim rulers.

25.9.2.2　　Integration into Qing Sovereignty

The Qing emphasized the transformation of these foreign lands into obedient territories of the empire:

"Ever since the Central Nation pacified and brought the Muslims to submission, they have become servants of the emperor who rules all under heaven."^329

This reflects how the Qing restructured governance in Turkistan, subordinating it to the central imperial administration while presenting their rule as a civilizing mission.

25.9.2.3　　Using Local Leaders to Consolidate Power

The Qing strategically reinstated Burhan al-Din and Khoja Jahan as rulers to stabilize the region under their control. By doing so, they leveraged local Muslim leaders as tools for domination:

"The Heavenly Khan took pity on the Muslims' long period of disunity, and he returned Burhan al-Din, along with all the Muslims who had been kidnapped, as well as the Burut, to their native lands. Thus Burhan al-Din himself became khan in Kashgar, while Khoja Jahan became khan in Yarkent."^330

This manipulation ensured initial compliance from the population while the Qing consolidated their hold.

25.9.2.4　　Perceived Weakness and Dependence

The narrative highlights the perceived inadequacies of Muslim governance and military strength, framing Qing intervention as necessary and benevolent:

"The Muslims are by nature docile and weak. The pasturage in their territory was also of poor quality, and their horses were not strong. Thus, they could not easily resist [the Burut (Kyrgyz) raids]."^331

Such descriptions portray the Muslim rulers as incapable of maintaining order, further justifying Qing domination.

25.9.2.5 Suppression of Rebellion

When the reinstated leaders, Burhan al-Din and Khoja Jahan, rebelled against Qing authority, the empire responded decisively:

"General Jaohūi led an army and pursued the rebel Burhan al-Din and the others as far as Badakhshan... and wiped them out."^332

This demonstrates the Qing's readiness to eliminate those who opposed their authority, reinforcing their dominance in the region.

· · ·· · · · ·· · · · ·· ·· · · ·· ·· ·· · · ··· · · ·· · · ··· · · · · · ·· · · · · · · ··
·· ·· · · · · ·· · ·· · · · ···

The fall of East Turkistan to the Qing Empire in 1759 was the result of multiple factors that weakened the region's ability to defend against foreign invasion. From internal divisions and leadership weaknesses to external pressures from neighboring powers, several elements converged to erode East Turkistan's independence.

25.10.1 Fragmentation of Local Power

The decline of the Yarkent Khanate created a power vacuum in East Turkistan, which was soon filled by competing factions within the Khoja family, primarily the Aq Taghlik (White Mountain) and Qara Taghlik (Black Mountain) factions. These internal rivalries prevented the establishment of a unified authority capable of resisting foreign threats, leaving East Turkistan susceptible to becoming a battleground for other powers, including the Dzungars and, eventually, the Qing Empire. Mahmud ibn Wali, a 17th-century historian from Balkh, documented the region's internal weaknesses, observing that the divisions within the Khoja family and among local rulers significantly destabilized the region and made it more vulnerable to foreign intervention.^333

25.10.2 Weaknesses within Khoja Leadership

Although the Khoja leaders held considerable spiritual and political influence, their ability to maintain stable rule was undermined by factional infighting and a reliance on external allies, such as the Dzungars. This dependence on non-Muslim foreign powers alienated the Uyghur population, as alliances with the Dzungars were often seen as compromising both Turkic and Islamic values. Many viewed the Khojas as prioritizing personal ambitions over the welfare of the region, weakening popular support for a unified resistance. Mahmud ibn Wali criticized these alliances as strategic missteps that further divided the local population and eroded the credibility of Khoja leaders.^334

25.10.3 Dzungar Domination

The Dzungar Mongols initially supported Afaq Khoja, a prominent Aq Taghlik leader, as a means to exert influence over East Turkistan. However, the Dzungars soon imposed direct control, establishing an oppressive rule that created widespread suffering and resentment. This weakened the region's autonomy and ability to resist further invasions. When the Qing defeated the Dzungars in the 1750s, East Turkistan was left vulnerable and ill-prepared for another conquest. By the time the Qing arrived, the Uyghur population's resources, strength, and endurance were severely depleted.^335

25.10.4 Qing Expansion and Strategic Interests

During the 18th century, the Qing Empire pursued an aggressive expansion into Central Asia, aiming to secure trade routes and stabilize its borders. Following the defeat of the Dzungars, the Qing saw East Turkistan as a strategically significant frontier region that needed to be brought under imperial control. Official Qing accounts attributed their victory to superior military strength, advanced weaponry, and the internal divisions that had weakened local resistance.^336

25.10.5 Conclusion

The fall of East Turkistan resulted from a convergence of internal divisions, weaknesses in leadership, foreign domination under the Dzungars, and Qing expansionism. These factors—combined with the perspectives of historians from various backgrounds—paint a complex picture of a region struggling with both internal discord and external pressures. The legacy of the Khojas' resistance and the region's eventual fall to the Qing underscores the significance of unity and autonomy in the face of foreign intervention and serves as a historical lesson on the impact of strategic errors and internal fragmentation.

Notes

325.   Mark Brophy, "An Early Manchu Account of the Western Regions," *Central Asiatic Journal* 60, no. 1-2 (2016-2017): 35-39.

326. Ibid., 36.
327. Ibid., 39.
328. Ibid., 36.
329. Ibid., 39.
330. Ibid., 35.
331. Ibid., 39.
332. Ibid., 36.
333. James Millward, *Eurasian Crossroads: A History of Xinjiang* (New York: Columbia University Press, 2007).
334. Mahmud ibn Wali, as referenced in James Millward, *Eurasian Crossroads: A History of Xinjiang* (New York: Columbia University Press, 2007) and Hodong Kim, *Holy War in China: The Muslim Rebellion and State in Chinese Central Asia, 1864–1877* (Stanford, CA: Stanford University Press, 2004).
335. Ibid.
336. Michael Dillon, *Xinjiang: China's Muslim Far Northwest* (New York: Routledge, 2004).

From Empires to Exile: A Brief Uyghur History

The descendants of Afaq Khoja continued their fight for Uyghur independence in East Turkistan after the Qing conquest of 1759, but their efforts ultimately failed due to a combination of internal and external challenges. While the Khojas mounted several uprisings over the next century, each was eventually suppressed by the Qing, which had both military superiority and strategic leverage over the region.^337

• • •• • • • • • •• • • •• •• •• • • • •••• • ••• • • • • •

In the 1820s, Jahangir Khoja, a descendant of Afaq Khoja, launched a major rebellion against the Qing Empire. Seeking to reclaim his family's former kingdom in the Tarim Basin, Jahangir appealed to both political and religious sentiments, drawing support from the local Uyghur population and the Kokand Khanate. Jahangir's family lineage and his status in the Sufi order (White Mountain faction) gave him substantial legitimacy among the Uyghurs, who viewed him as a rightful heir to the region.^338

With support from Kokand, Jahangir captured key cities, including Kashgar, Yarkent, and Khotan, establishing brief control over parts of East Turkistan. However, the Qing mobilized a large force, reportedly numbering 100,000 to 200,000 troops, under General Changling to suppress the rebellion.^339 Despite determined resistance, Jahangir's forces were ultimately overwhelmed by the Qing's superior numbers and resources. In 1827, Jahangir was captured, taken to Beijing, and executed, marking the end of his attempt to restore independent rule in East Turkistan.^340

• • •• • • •••• • • •• •• •• • • • •••• • ••• • • • • •

Jahangir's son, Wali Khoja, continued the family's struggle for independence in the 1850s, leading another uprising against Qing rule. Capitalizing on anti-Qing sentiment and leveraging his family's spiritual authority, Wali Khoja gained the support of southern East Turkistan's Muslim population. He received military aid from the Kokand Khanate, whose rulers sought to weaken Qing influence in the region. With this external support, Wali

Khoja captured major cities like Kashgar, Yarkent, and Khotan, briefly establishing a semi-independent rule.^341

However, Wali Khoja's successes were short-lived. The Qing, determined to maintain control over East Turkistan, launched a counteroffensive that recaptured the rebel-held cities. The Qing's military superiority, combined with Wali Khoja's limited resources and reliance on Kokand's inconsistent support, led to the failure of the rebellion. Wali Khoja either died in battle or was captured and executed, marking the definitive end of his campaign.^342

Several factors contributed to the repeated failure of the Khoja-led rebellions:

- **Qing Military Superiority:** The Qing Empire had a large, well-equipped army with advanced weaponry, including artillery and firearms. This gave them a significant advantage over the Khoja forces, who were less well-armed and struggled to sustain prolonged campaigns.^343
- **Lack of Unity:** Internal divisions within the Khoja family, particularly between the Aq Taghlik (White Mountain) and Qara Taghlik (Black Mountain) factions, prevented a unified resistance. These rivalries fragmented Uyghur support and weakened the overall effectiveness of their campaigns.^344
- **Limited External Support:** While the Khojas received some aid from the Kokand Khanate, this support was inconsistent and insufficient to counter the Qing's overwhelming resources. Kokand itself was a relatively small state with limited military power, which constrained its ability to provide sustained assistance.^345

The Qing Empire was at its peak during the conquest of East Turkistan and employed both military and diplomatic strategies to secure control over the region:

- **Military Strength:** The Qing army was well-organized, with forces composed of Manchu, Mongol, and Han Chinese soldiers. Their advanced weaponry and strategic approach allowed them to effectively quell resistance and maintain authority in the region.^346
- **Strategic Alliances:** The Qing used a combination of rewards and punishments to secure loyalty from local leaders, offering incentives to those who pledged allegiance while swiftly suppressing uprisings. This strategy allowed the Qing to establish lasting control over the diverse and expansive region of East Turkistan.

The legacy of the Khoja family's resistance remains an important part of Uyghur history, symbolizing the enduring struggle for self-determination. Though their uprisings were ultimately unsuccessful, their efforts are remembered as part of the broader resistance against foreign domination in East Turkistan.

Notes

337. Michael Dillon, *Xinjiang: China's Muslim Far Northwest* (New York: Routledge, 2004).
338. Hodong Kim, *Holy War in China: The Muslim Rebellion and State in Chinese Central Asia, 1864–1877* (Stanford, CA: Stanford University Press, 2004).
339. Musa Sayrami, *Tārīkh-i amniyya*, as cited in James Millward, *Eurasian Crossroads* (New York: Columbia University Press, 2007).
340. Ibid.
341. Michael Dillon, *Xinjiang: China's Muslim Far Northwest* (New York: Routledge, 2004).
342. Ibid.
343. Ibid.
344. Ibid.
345. Ibid.
346. Ibid.

Uyghur Struggles for Regaining Independence: The Rise and Fall of the Yettishahr

Muhammad Yakub Beg or Yakub Beg (1820–1877) was a prominent leader who established an independent state in East Turkistan during a period of intense political upheaval. Though initially serving as a military commander in the Khanate of Kokand, his reign was marked by complex diplomatic relations, military conquests, and eventual downfall. Yakub Beg's state, Yettishahr, was recognized by the three major empires of the time—the Ottoman Empire, the British Empire, and the Russian Empire—and he entered into diplomatic agreements with each, a rare achievement for a regional leader.^347

In 1864, amidst the widespread uprisings against Qing rule in East Turkistan, the Kucha Rebellion erupted as a powerful assertion of Muslim discontent. Oppressive taxation, forced labor, and cultural suppression had long bred resentment among Uyghur and other Muslim populations. Rashuddin Khoja emerged as a central figure during this upheaval, leading the rebellion in Kucha and expelling Qing officials from the city.^348 Under his leadership, the city became a rallying point for resistance, inspiring revolts in neighboring regions.

Rashuddin Khoja's ambitions extended beyond Kucha. His first campaign targeted Aqsu, but his forces, led by Sayyid Khatib Khoja, were repelled, suffering significant losses. Undeterred, Rashuddin Khoja regrouped and launched a second assault, successfully capturing Aqsu under the command of Sayyid Jamaluddin Khoja. Buoyed by this victory, he set his sights eastward, targeting Qarashahr and Turpan. By 1865, his forces had dismantled Qing defenses in Qarashahr, opening the path to Turpan, where his military and spiritual leadership enabled further gains against Qing authority.^349

Despite these successes, Rashuddin Khoja's campaigns highlighted the fractured nature of the resistance. His attempts to seize Kashgar in late 1864 revealed internal divisions and external betrayals, particularly from Siddiq Beg of the Kipchaqs, who ambushed his forces. These setbacks emphasized the challenges of uniting the diverse factions opposing Qing rule.^350

By 1865, the region was a patchwork of competing Muslim leaders and fragmented authority, destabilized by rebellion but lacking a cohesive power. It was in this volatile environment that Yakub Beg, a skilled commander from Kokand, entered the scene. Recognizing the opportunity presented by the disarray, Yakub began forging alliances and consolidating power. Rashuddin Khoja's campaigns, though pivotal in weakening Qing rule, ultimately set the stage for Yakub Beg's rise. His efforts laid the groundwork for Yakub's unification of East Turkistan under the Yettishahr state, a turning point in the region's history.^351 Rashuddin's legacy thus serves as a bridge between rebellion and unification, marking the tumultuous years leading to Yakub Beg's ascent to power in the mid-1860s.

• • •• •• • ••• ••• • •• • ••• • •• • • •• • •• • •• • ••• ••• •• •• • ••• • •• •• •• •

Yakub Beg's entry into East Turkistan was facilitated by the Khojas, descendants of the influential Sufi leader Afaq Khoja, who invited him to aid their resistance against Qing rule. The Khojas hoped to benefit from Yakub Beg's military expertise and his ties to the Kokand Khanate. This invitation came at a time of intense regional instability, with the Qing Empire struggling to maintain control due to internal rebellions like the Dungan Revolt and competing Muslim factions vying for dominance. The Kucha Rebellion and simultaneous uprisings in other cities such as Kashgar, Yarkent, and Khotan erupted as Uyghur and other Muslim groups resisted Qing rule in response to oppressive taxation, forced labor, and cultural suppression. Recognizing the opportunity presented by the weakened local power structures and external threats, Yakub Beg capitalized on the chaos to establish himself as a powerful figure in the region.^352

Night interview with Yakub Beg, Amir of YettiShahr, 1868	Muhammad Yakub Beg Amir of YettiShahr

• • •• • • • • • ••• • • • • ••• ••• • •••• • • • • ••• •• • • •

  By 1865, Yakub Beg entered Kashgar at the Khojas' request but soon marginalized their influence to consolidate power under his leadership. His state, widely known as Yettishahr (meaning "Seven Cities"), initially included the major cities of the Tarim Basin: Kashgar, Yarkent, Khotan, Aksu, Kucha, Qarashahr, and Uchturpan. Over time, his domain expanded to include Turpan, a strategically vital city north of the Tengri Mountains, which acted as a gateway between eastern China and the Tarim Basin. The state operated as an Islamic polity, with Yakub Beg assuming the title of Amir and centralizing authority through military administration. He maintained control through alliances with local elites, tribal leaders, and religious authorities, integrating Islamic law into his governance. Despite its initial success, the state's cohesion relied on Yakub Beg's ability to balance the diverse ethnic and religious groups within his domain.^353

From Empires to Exile: A Brief Uyghur History

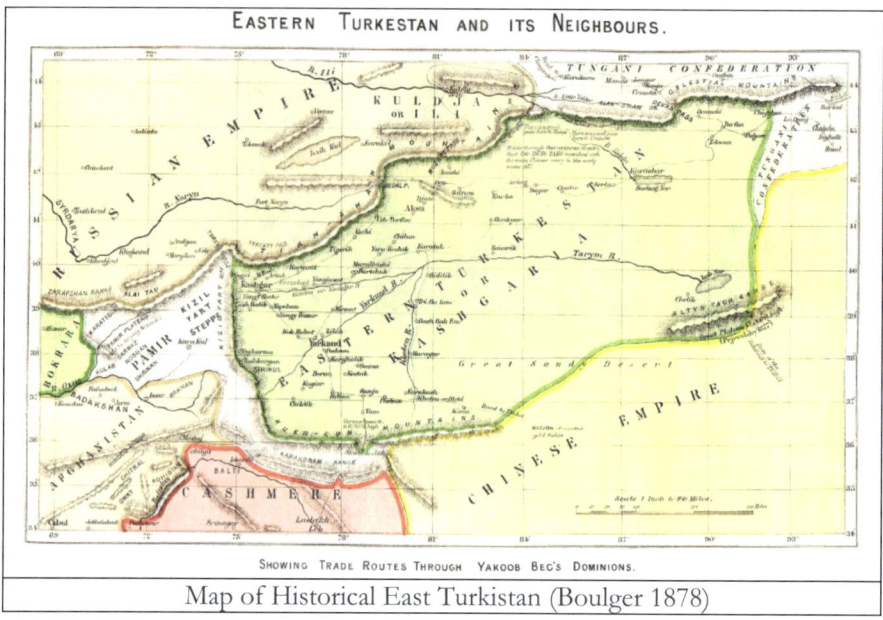

Map of Historical East Turkistan (Boulger 1878)

• •• • •• •• • ••• •• • • • • • •• ••• • •• •• •• • •• ••• • ••• •

One of Yakub Beg's most remarkable achievements was gaining recognition and forming diplomatic relations with three of the most powerful empires of his time—the Russian Empire, the Ottoman Empire, and the British Empire. This gave him both legitimacy and strategic advantages, although the support he received from these empires was primarily symbolic and did not provide the material resources he needed for long-term stability.^354

The Ottoman Empire, which viewed itself as the protector of Muslims globally, officially recognized Yakub Beg as the "Governor of Kashgar" in the 1870s. This recognition elevated Yakub Beg's status as a legitimate ruler in the eyes of the broader Muslim world. Sultan Abdulaziz and later Sultan Abdulhamid II supported Yakub Beg's rule diplomatically, although they provided little military or financial aid. The Ottomans even bestowed titles and honors upon him, which Yakub Beg used to strengthen his rule and enhance his standing among the Muslim populations of Kashgaria.^355

During the period known as the "Great Game," the rivalry between the British Empire and the Russian Empire for control over Central Asia, Yakub Beg became a key figure of interest for British diplomats. The British, wary of Russian expansion in Central Asia, saw Yakub Beg's state as a potential buffer zone against Russian influence. British envoys like Robert Shaw, who visited Yettishahr (Kashgaria), reported on the region's political

135

situation and the potential for establishing trade relations with Yakub Beg. While Yakub Beg and the British did not formalize a military alliance, he was recognized by British officials, and his state was seen as a valuable player in the broader geopolitical contest between Britain and Russia.^356

The Russian Empire recognized Yakub Beg's Yettishahr diplomatically during his reign, mainly due to their strategic interests in Central Asia. Though Russia did not provide direct support, they allowed limited trade and maintained diplomatic contacts with Yakub Beg's government. However, by the time of the Qing reconquest, Russia shifted its stance, agreeing not to interfere with Qing efforts to reclaim East Turkistan. This was part of a broader geopolitical understanding between Russia and the Qing, solidified by treaties like the Treaty of Livadia (1879), which delineated spheres of influence and recognized Qing sovereignty over East Turkistan.^357

Yakub Beg also contributed significantly to the infrastructure of Yettishahr, constructing public baths (hammams), caravanserais, and other facilities that improved trade and social services, reflecting his commitment to regional development and governance.

YettiShahr Army

• • •• • •• •• •• • • ••• • •• • ••• • ••• •••• • ••

The Qing Empire's military campaign to reconquer East Turkistan from Yakub Beg began in 1876, led by General Zuo Zongtang, and involved a sizable force, though exact numbers vary. According to historical estimates, Zuo Zongtang commanded an army of approximately 60,000 to 100,000 troops at its peak, which included regular Qing forces, provincial troops, and logistics personnel.^358 This military force was well-equipped and funded by the Qing government, which had stabilized its internal situation after years of rebellion and now sought to reassert control over East Turkistan.

As the Qing forces advanced methodically from Beijing through Korla, Qarashahr, and into Toqsun, Yakub Beg attempted to organize a defense. Spies such as In'am Khoja Ishan were sent to assess the advancing Chinese. Their reports painted a grim picture: *"The Chinese are innumerably, endlessly many. One cannot even see where their banners begin or where they end. These must be the soldiers whom the Emperor of China ordered hither."*

This revelation of the overwhelming size of the Qing forces shattered morale among Yakub Beg's ranks. Attempts at diplomacy, including sparing captured Chinese officers and granting them stipends, failed to secure peace.^359 Meanwhile, mistrust grew among Yakub Beg's commanders, leading to the banishment of their families and further weakening unity within his forces. Defections and secret communications with the Qing undermined Yakub Beg's position. His continued reluctance to engage the advancing Qing army allowed them to proceed largely unopposed, contributing to the collapse of defenses and the fragmentation of his forces.

• • •• • • • • • • •• • • •• •• •• •• • •• •• •• • • • ••

Skirmishes, such as the Battle of Dabanchi, saw initial success for Yakub Beg's troops under Niyaz Toqsaba, who commanded 2,000 soldiers. Despite killing 1,000 Qing troops in a counterattack, Yakub Beg's repeated orders to cease fire resulted in the loss of this strategic position. Qing reinforcements overwhelmed the defenders, capturing many soldiers and leaving Yakub Beg's forces weakened and demoralized.^360

Meanwhile, Haqq Quli Beg, stationed in Toqsun, ordered the burning of granaries filled with provisions that could have sustained Yakub Beg's forces for years, and retreated to Korla. Around the same time, the Chinese occupied Turpan and Toqsun, capturing the remaining abandoned supplies. These resources, including grain, fodder, and firewood, significantly bolstered the Qing forces while leaving Yakub Beg's troops without critical sustenance. The retreat without engagement highlighted the strategic disarray among his commanders.^361

The Battle of Dabanchi was a key early confrontation between Yakub Beg's forces and the advancing Qing army. Dabanchi, located on an important route between southern regions and the rest of the region, was a strategic stronghold that, if defended successfully, could have slowed or even stopped the Qing's advance. Yakub Beg's forces initially gained the upper hand in this battle, using the terrain to their advantage and pushing back the Qing troops. Despite this early momentum, Yakub Beg made the controversial decision to order his troops not to shoot during a critical phase of the battle. This decision, coupled with his retreat without fighting, was seen as a significant strategic mistake.^362

By abandoning key defensive points such as Turpan and Lokchun, Yakub Beg allowed the Qing forces to advance uncontested, capturing these cities with minimal resistance. His reluctance to fight further demoralized his troops, who were already struggling with low morale due to earlier retreats and defeats. The retreat also encouraged desertions and betrayals within his ranks, as local leaders and commanders lost faith in Yakub Beg's leadership, hastening the fall of his independent state.^363

At Qarashahr, Yakub Beg and his commanders regrouped with a sizable force, including 30,000 cavalry and his personal guard of 3,000, while swiftly reconstructing a fortress. However, hesitation and lack of unity among the commanders stalled decisive action, leaving the region vulnerable to the advancing Qing forces.^364

Yakub Beg's reluctance to engage the Qing directly and the disunity among his commanders accelerated the fall of his regime. His temper and erratic behavior further alienated his officers. During a critical moment in Qarashahr, Yakub Beg violently lashed out at Mullah Kamaluddin Mirza, an incident that symbolized his deteriorating control.^365

By 1877, Yakub Beg was in Qarashahr, one of his last strongholds, as the Qing forces, led by General Zuo Zongtang, advanced steadily westward to reclaim East Turkistan. On April 28, 1877, Yakub Beg died under suspicious circumstances. Historical accounts suggest he was poisoned by a servant bribed by Niyaz Hakim Beg, a rival seeking to end his rule. Reports state that Yakub Beg drank poisoned tea, recited "*Oh, Messenger of God!*" three times, and collapsed.^366 Whether the poisoning was the result of internal betrayal or a strategy to appease the advancing Qing forces remains unclear.

Yakub Beg's death marked the beginning of the rapid disintegration of his state. Without his unifying leadership, the region descended into chaos. Cities such as Kashgar and Yarkent fragmented into rival factions, weakening efforts to mount a coordinated defense against the Qing. Taking advantage of this disunity, General Zuo Zongtang's forces swiftly reconquered the region, city by city. By the end of 1877, all of East Turkistan had fallen back under Qing control, marking the end of Yakub Beg's brief reign and the dissolution of Kashgaria.^367–368

Yakub Beg's legacy is a complex one, shaped by both admiration and criticism. Contemporary observers, including historians, travelers, and diplomats, had varied opinions of his leadership:^368

Musa Sayrami, a local historian, offered a detailed and nuanced view of Yakub Beg's reign. He praised Yakub Beg for his military abilities and his success in uniting a fractured region under a single rule during a period of chaos. However, Sayrami also criticized Yakub Beg's increasingly autocratic governance. Heavy taxation, forced conscription, and harsh treatment of local populations, particularly the Dungans, led to widespread discontent. Sayrami argued that these oppressive policies ultimately contributed to Yakub Beg's downfall.^369

British observers like Robert Shaw, who traveled to Kashgaria and documented Yakub Beg's rule, acknowledged his skill as a military leader and administrator. Shaw noted that Yakub Beg had managed to bring stability to the region for a time and establish trade relations with foreign powers. However, Shaw also pointed out that Yakub Beg's state lacked the institutional strength and internal cohesion needed to withstand the Qing's eventual reconquest.^370

Ottoman officials viewed Yakub Beg as a valiant Muslim ruler resisting non-Muslim domination. While they had little direct involvement in his affairs, the Ottomans supported his claim to govern Kashgaria, and his symbolic significance as a Muslim leader extended beyond his military achievements.^371

• • •• • • • • •• ••• • • • •• • •• •• • • • •

Several factors contributed to Yakub Beg's defeat and the collapse of his independent state:^372

Qing Military Superiority: The Qing forces, after consolidating power in the wake of internal rebellions, were able to mount a well-organized and well-equipped campaign to retake East Turkistan. Led by General Zuo Zongtang, the Qing forces had superior numbers, resources, and logistical support.

Internal Discontent and Betrayal: Yakub Beg's autocratic rule alienated many of his supporters. Heavy taxation, forced conscription, and the persecution of certain Muslim groups, including the Dungans, led to widespread dissatisfaction. The final betrayal, likely involving Hakim Beg, reflected the deep divisions within Yakub Beg's camp.

Loss of External Support: The annexation of the Kokand Khanate by Russia in 1876 deprived Yakub Beg of a critical ally. Although he had diplomatic recognition from the Ottoman Empire and Britain, neither provided the material support necessary to fend off the Qing military campaign.

Fragmentation After His Death: The political fragmentation that followed Yakub Beg's death made it easier for the Qing to reconquer the region. Local warlords and religious leaders fought among themselves for control, weakening the ability to resist the Qing.

Autocratic Governance: Yakub Beg's reliance on coercion and military force, rather than building popular support or sustainable governance structures, eroded the foundations of his state. His increasingly harsh policies alienated the very people he needed to maintain power.

• • •• • • • • • • •• • • • •• •• • •• ••• • • • • ••• • •• • ••• •••• • •• • • ••••

Molla Musa Sayrami, a prominent Uyghur historian and contemporary of Yakub Beg, provides a critical yet balanced account in his book *Tārīkh-i Ḥamīdī* (The History of Hamidi). In the book, Sayrami mentions a rumor that Yakub Beg killed 50,000 people in Khotan, but this claim is highly questionable for several reasons. While some Western sources have suggested Yakub Beg's forces were relatively small, with estimates ranging from 10,000 to 15,000 soldiers, Sayrami himself notes that Yakub Beg commanded forces of over 30,000 at key moments, such as the regrouping at Qarashahr. Even with such numbers, carrying out a massacre of 50,000 civilians in a single campaign remains logistically improbable. Additionally, there are no credible historical records indicating that Yakub Beg deliberately targeted civilians during his campaigns. His military actions were primarily focused on suppressing rebellious factions and rival elites rather than engaging in indiscriminate violence against the general population.^373

Yakub Beg's origins in the Kokand Khanate have led some to speculate that he may have favored Kokand allies or discriminated against the local population in East Turkistan. However, historical evidence does not support the claim that he systematically marginalized the indigenous population. On the contrary, Yakub Beg relied heavily on local Uyghur, Kyrgyz, and Kazakh leaders, as well as religious authorities, to consolidate his rule and legitimize his governance. By aligning himself with Islamic values and presenting himself as a defender of Islam against Qing domination, Yakub Beg garnered significant respect among the local population. While his rule was undoubtedly strict and involved harsh measures to suppress dissent, Yakub Beg was generally respected for his ability to restore order and defend the region from external threats.^374

The narrative of widespread civilian massacres, including the alleged 50,000 deaths in Khotan, appears to have been influenced by propaganda from his opponents, such as the Qing Empire, or later interpretations seeking to discredit his leadership. In conclusion, Yakub Beg's rule was characterized by military pragmatism, respect for local customs, and strategic alliances rather than indiscriminate violence or ethnic discrimination. These qualities were crucial in maintaining his legitimacy and control over the diverse and volatile region of East Turkistan. The lack of evidence for civilian massacres and his reliance on local support challenge the portrayal of Yakub Beg as a ruthless or oppressive ruler.^375

Qing General Zuo Zongtang's strategic approach in defeating Yakub Beg and his forces during the Qing reconquest of East Turkistan was marked by a deep understanding of local dynamics, Yakub Beg's weaknesses, and the multi-ethnic composition of the region. Zuo Zongtang's strategy involved not only military tactics but also psychological and social maneuvers, which played a significant role in Yakub Beg's downfall. Below are the primary strategies he used:

Sowing Division within Yakub Beg's Forces: Zuo Zongtang capitalized on the ethnic and ideological diversity within Yakub Beg's ranks. Yakub Beg's army included a mix of Uyghurs, Kazakhs, Kyrgyz, and Chinese Muslims (Hui). By exploiting pre-existing tensions between these groups, Zuo's forces spread distrust, leading to fractures within Yakub Beg's support base.^376

Winning Over Chinese Muslims (Hui) Based on Regional Ties: Recognizing that Chinese Muslims had historical and regional ties to the Qing, Zuo worked to persuade them that their interests aligned more with the Qing government than with Yakub Beg's regime. He emphasized shared heritage and reassured the Hui that they would be treated well under Qing rule.^377

Using City-based Loyalty to Divide and Control: Zuo Zongtang was familiar with the local loyalties of various cities and regions within East Turkistan. His strategy extended to turning other local powers against Kashgar, Yakub Beg's stronghold, by capitalizing on longstanding rivalries and regional identities. Zuo played on the resentment felt by nearby cities like Yarkent and Khotan, subtly promoting the idea that Kashgar's dominance under Yakub Beg threatened their autonomy.^378

Encouraging Defection and Desertion: Zuo Zongtang was well aware of the discontent among Yakub Beg's troops, especially among those conscripted under duress or facing low morale due to harsh conditions. He launched propaganda campaigns aimed at encouraging Yakub Beg's soldiers to desert. Qing officials offered incentives to those who defected, such as financial rewards, the promise of reintegration, or even positions within the Qing forces.^379

Using Psychological Warfare and Rumors: Zuo's forces spread rumors to undermine Yakub Beg's authority, suggesting he was losing favor, weakening, or on the verge of defeat. These rumors eroded Yakub Beg's aura of invincibility and sowed fear and doubt among his soldiers and allies.^380

Leveraging Qing Military Superiority and Logistics: While Yakub Beg's forces were often scattered and reliant on local resources, Zuo Zongtang carefully managed supply lines and brought advanced artillery and reinforcements from inland China. His disciplined logistics enabled the Qing army to sustain prolonged campaigns in the harsh terrain of East Turkistan, which further demoralized Yakub Beg's forces, who faced dwindling resources and unreliable supply chains.^381

Strategic Alliances with Local Leaders and Religious Authorities: Zuo Zongtang knew that religious and community leaders held significant influence in East Turkistan. By negotiating with influential leaders and promising favorable treatment under Qing rule, Zuo won over several key figures who either withdrew support from Yakub Beg or helped rally local populations against him.^382

Through these tactics, Zuo Zongtang effectively dismantled Yakub Beg's power base, capitalizing on the regional divisions and understanding the dynamics that held Yakub Beg's coalition together. His nuanced approach demonstrates his strategic intelligence and deep knowledge of East Turkistan's complex social fabric, ultimately leading to Yakub Beg's defeat and the Qing reconquest of the region.

Notes:

347. For Yakub Beg's background and state-building efforts, see Robert Barkley Shaw, *Kashgaria: Eastern Turkistan* (London: Trübner & Co., 1878); Musa Sayrami, *Tārīkh-i amniyya* (Kashgar: N.P., 1903).

348. Musa Sayrami and Eric Schluessel, "Introduction," in *The Tarikh-i Ḥamidi: A Late-Qing Uyghur History*, xv–xxx (Columbia University Press, 2023).

349. Accounts of Rashuddin Khoja's campaigns are documented in Michael Dillon, *Xinjiang: China's Muslim Far Northwest* (London: Routledge, 2004), 83–85.

350. Details of resistance struggles and their fragmentation are discussed in James A. Millward, *Eurasian Crossroads: A History of Xinjiang* (New York: Columbia University Press, 2007), 117–119.

351. On Yakub Beg's rise and unification efforts, see Musa Sayrami, *Tārīkh-i amniyya*; Peter Hopkirk, *The Great Game: On Secret Service in High Asia* (Oxford: Oxford University Press, 1992), 314–317.

352. Accounts of the Khojas' invitation and Yakub Beg's entry into East Turkistan are in Michael Dillon, *Xinjiang*, 92–95.

353. For descriptions of the Yettishahr state and its administration, see Shaw, *Kashgaria*, 62–64; Sayrami, *Tārīkh-i amniyya*.

354. Diplomatic relations between Yakub Beg's Yettishahr and other empires are examined in Peter Hopkirk, *The Great Game*, 314–320.

355. For details on Ottoman recognition and Yakub Beg's relationship with the Muslim world, see Zeki Velidi Togan, *Umumi Türk Tarihi* (Istanbul: Ismail Ağa, 1977), 204–207.

356. British perspectives on Yakub Beg and his state are analyzed in Robert Barkley Shaw, *Kashgaria*, 121–122.

357. Qing-Russian agreements and the Treaty of Livadia (1879) are discussed in Mark C. Elliott, *The Manchu Way: The Eight Banners and Ethnic Identity in Late Imperial China* (Stanford: Stanford University Press, 2001), 204.

358. On Zuo Zongtang's military campaign and Qing logistics, see Edward H. Kaplan, *The War against the Dungan Rebels* (Cambridge: Harvard University Press, 1990), 167–175.

359. Reports on the Qing forces' strength and Yakub Beg's attempts at defense are in James A. Millward, *Eurasian Crossroads*, 190–192.

360. Strategic errors and losses at the Battle of Dabanchi are discussed in Musa Sayrami, *Tārīkh-i amniyya*, 121–125.
361. Accounts of supply destruction and its impact on Yakub Beg's forces are in Michael Dillon, *Xinjiang*, 100–103.
362. On Yakub Beg's decisions during the Battle of Dabanchi, see David D. Wang, *Under the Soviet Shadow: The Yining Incident* (Hong Kong: Chinese University Press, 1999), 112.
363. Morale issues and defections in Yakub Beg's forces are detailed in Sayrami, *Tārīkh-i amniyya*, 127–130.
364. Attempts to regroup at Qarashahr and their failures are discussed in Shaw, *Kashgaria*, 122–123.
365. Incidents leading to Yakub Beg's loss of control are noted in Millward, *Eurasian Crossroads*, 195.
366. Historical accounts of Yakub Beg's death and suspicions of poisoning are in Sayrami, *Tārīkh-i amniyya*, 135.
367. The collapse of Kashgaria after Yakub Beg's death is examined in Shaw, *Kashgaria*, 123–126.
368. The Qing reconquest of Kashgaria and its implications are detailed in Kaplan, *The War against the Dungan Rebels*, 192–200.
369. Musa Sayrami, *Tārīkh-i Ḥamīdī* (The History of Hamidi), edited by Eric Schluessel, Columbia University Press, 2023.
370. Robert Barkley Shaw, *Kashgaria: Eastern Turkistan*, London: Trübner & Co., 1878.
371. Zeki Velidi Togan, *Umumi Türk Tarihi*, Istanbul: Ismail Ağa, 1977.
372. James A. Millward, *Eurasian Crossroads: A History of Xinjiang*, Columbia University Press, 2007.
373. Musa Sayrami and Eric Schluessel, in The Tarikh-i Ḥamidi: A Late-Qing Uyghur History, xv–xxx (Columbia University Press, 2023).
374. Michael Dillon, *Xinjiang: China's Muslim Far Northwest*, London: Routledge, 2004.
375. Musa Sayrami and Eric Schluessel, in The Tarikh-i Ḥamidi: A Late-Qing Uyghur History, xv–xxx (Columbia University Press, 2023).
376. Edward H. Kaplan, *The War against the Dungan Rebels*, Cambridge: Harvard University Press, 1990.
377. Mark C. Elliott, *The Manchu Way: The Eight Banners and Ethnic Identity in Late Imperial China*, Stanford University Press, 2001.
378. James A. Millward, *Eurasian Crossroads: A History of Xinjiang*, Columbia University Press, 2007.
379. Edward H. Kaplan, *The War against the Dungan Rebels*, Harvard University Press, 1990.
380. Musa Sayrami and Eric Schluessel, in The Tarikh-i Ḥamidi: A Late-Qing Uyghur History, xv–xxx (Columbia University Press, 2023).
381. Qing military logistics and superiority are documented in Kaplan, The War against the Dungan Rebels, 220.
382. James A. Millward, *Eurasian Crossroads: A History of Xinjiang*, Columbia University Press, 2007.

• • •• •• •• • • • •• • • • •••••• • • •• • • • • • • • • ••• • • •• • • • • • •

After the fall of the Yarkent Khanate, and subsequent fall of East Turkistan in 1759, the Kokand Khanate emerged as a critical supporter of East Turkistan, leveraging shared ethnic, historical, cultural, religious, and economic ties to aid Uyghur resistance against Qing rule. As a neighboring power, Kokand provided military, economic, and logistical support to Uyghur leaders, particularly members of the Khoja families, descendants of Afaq Khoja. These efforts were aimed at challenging Qing authority in southern East

Turkistan, reclaiming control over Kashgar and surrounding areas, and protecting Kokand's strategic interests in regional trade and influence.^383

The Kokand Khanate served as a sanctuary for Uyghur leaders fleeing Qing repression. From its base in the Ferghana Valley, Kokand provided resources, refuge, and military aid to fuel resistance efforts, especially during uprisings led by prominent Khoja figures such as Jahangir Khoja in the 1820s and Wali Khan in the 1850s. The valley's role as an economic hub allowed the movement of arms, goods, and resources necessary to sustain the uprisings, while also facilitating broader connections between East Turkistan and Central Asia.^384

This cross-border cooperation strengthened the cultural and political bonds between the Uyghur people and Central Asian communities. It also represented a broader regional solidarity against Qing dominance, as other Central Asian powers supported trade networks and asylum for displaced Uyghurs. However, these alliances were not purely altruistic; Kokand sought to expand its influence, secure critical trade routes, and counterbalance Qing power in the region.^385

Migration estimates indicate that tens of thousands of people fled East Turkistan to Kokand and Central Asia during key periods of conflict, such as the Qing conquest of 1759 and the subsequent 19th-century uprisings. The displacement intensified after the defeat of Yakub Beg in 1877, when thousands of his followers and other Turkic groups escaped Qing reprisals. Over the century, the total number of migrants from East Turkistan to Central Asia likely reached hundreds of thousands. This migration significantly reshaped the demographics of both East Turkistan and Central Asia, with refugees integrating into the social and economic fabric of the Kokand Khanate and the Ferghana Valley. These movements solidified cross-regional ties, with Uyghur refugees contributing to the resistance against Qing rule while maintaining their cultural identity.^386

· · ·· · · · ·· · · · ···· · · · ···· · · · · ··

The Kumul Khanate became increasingly distinct from the Yarkent Khanate during the late 17th century, as the Dzungars began exerting influence over southern East Turkistan, including Yarkent. After the collapse of the Yarkent Khaganate in the early 18th century, descendants of Said Khan, a ruler from the Chagatai lineage, fled or were displaced across the region.^387 Some members of this royal family settled in Kumul, where the Qing Empire recognized them as local rulers.^388 Leveraging their prestigious lineage, the descendants of Said Khan governed Kumul as a semi-autonomous vassal state under Qing suzerainty, giving rise to the Kumul Khaganate, which lasted until its abolition by

Republican China in 1930.^389 This arrangement allowed the khaganate to maintain its authority while paying tribute to the Qing.

The last Khan of Kumul, Maksud Shah, died in 1930, leading to a period of instability in the region. This event contributed to the Kumul Rebellion in 1931, which sparked broader unrest across East Turkistan as local populations resisted Chinese warlord rule.^390

• • •• • • • • •••••• • ••• • • ••

The mid-19th century was marked by widespread instability across East Turkistan, culminating in the Uyghur, Kazakh and Dungan rebellions of 1864. These uprisings were fueled by grievances against Qing administration and economic hardships. In the Ili Valley, the rebellion led to the establishment of the Ili Sultanate, a short-lived political entity led by local Uyghur and other Turkic muslim leaders aiming to create an independent state.^391

The Ili Sultanate sought to protect not only its Uyghur core population but also neighboring Kazakhs, who faced displacement and external pressures from the expanding Russian Empire. The leadership attempted to unify the Muslim populations of the region, including sedentary farmers and nomadic herders, to resist Qing incursions and Russian expansion.^392 However, the Sultanate was hampered by internal divisions, resource limitations, and the challenges of maintaining cohesion among its diverse constituents.

Ala Khan Sultan, the Ruler of Ili Sultanate, captured in a photograph taken in 1864

Despite its efforts to assert autonomy and protect vulnerable communities, the Ili Sultanate was weakened by external threats and internal instability, leaving it vulnerable to foreign intervention.^393

27.16.1 Russian Occupation (1871–1881)

In 1871, the Russian Empire invaded and overthrew the Ili Sultanate. The Russians justified their intervention by citing border security concerns and the need to protect Russian Central Asia from the instability in East Turkistan. However, their occupation extended beyond their initial claims, disrupting the region's traditional political and economic structures. ^394

During the occupation, the Russian administration introduced new governance policies, reorganizing land distribution and taxation systems. This created tensions among the Uyghur and Kazakh populations, some of whom cooperated with Russian authorities while others resisted foreign rule. The Russians also encouraged migration from their controlled territories in Central Asia, altering the region's demographics.

The Russian occupation lasted a decade and ended with the Treaty of Saint Petersburg in 1881, which returned most of the Ili Valley to Qing control. However, the Russians retained certain border territories and secured trade privileges, marking a lasting geopolitical shift in the region.^395

27.16.2　After the Qing Reconquest

The Qing Empire reoccupied the Ili region following the Russian withdrawal but abandoned the semi-autonomous governance structures that had previously defined the area. Instead, they implemented direct rule, integrating the region more tightly into the imperial framework. The Qing military presence increased significantly, and land policies favored Han and Manchu settlers, creating further discontent among the local Muslim populations.

The Ili Valley became a key Qing military and administrative center, aligned with broader efforts to stabilize East Turkistan and prevent further uprisings. This process culminated in the formal designation of East Turkistan as the province of "Xinjiang" in 1884, meaning "New Frontier," further solidifying Qing control over the region. ^396

27.16.3　Legacy of the Ili Sultanate

The Ili Sultanate represents a critical moment in the region's history, reflecting the aspirations of its Uyghur population for self-rule and unity during a period of political upheaval. Its failure underscores the challenges of governing a multi-ethnic frontier region amidst competing internal and external pressures. The legacy of the Sultanate highlights the enduring struggle of the Ili region's inhabitants to navigate the complexities of empire, autonomy, and cultural identity.^397

• • •• • • •• •• •••• • •••• • • ••• • • • • ••• • ••• • •• • •••• ••• • • • •• • •• • •• •• •

27.17.1　Qing Scholar Official Wei Yuan

In his *Military History of the Western Regions* (1844), Qing scholar Wei Yuan chronicled the Qing's campaigns in East Turkistan. Wei emphasized the Qing military's organizational and logistical superiority, while also noting the fragmentation among the local Turkic rulers, particularly the Khojas. He viewed the conquest as a civilizing mission aimed at stabilizing a chaotic frontier and portrayed Qing rule as superior to previous local powers like the Dzungars and Khojas.^398

27.17.2　Contemporary Central Asian Perspectives on the Fall

The Kokand Khanate, a Central Asian Muslim state with cultural ties to the Turkic population of East Turkistan, had its own perspective on the region's fall. During the 19th-century Khoja rebellions, leaders like Jahangir Khoja and Wali Khan sought support from Kokand against the Qing. However, Kokand's support was limited by its own instability and the growing influence of both Qing and Russian empires. Kokand viewed the fall of East Turkistan as a loss for the broader Turkic and Islamic world and lamented its inability to provide effective military aid.^399

27.17.3   38.5.3 Later Interpretations and Legacy

Many modern historians interpret the fall of East Turkistan as part of the broader decline of Central Asian powers under imperial pressure from the Qing Empire and the Russian Empire. The fragmentation and weakening of native Turkic states like the Yarkent Khanate and the Khoja rulers left the region vulnerable to the expanding influence of China and Russia.^400

James Millward, a contemporary historian of Central Asia, argues that the fall of East Turkistan reflects a broader pattern of imperial expansion in the 18th and 19th centuries. He emphasizes the internal divisions among the Khojas, Dzungars, and other regional powers as key factors in the region's vulnerability to Qing conquest, also noting the Qing strategy of indirect control.^401

Notes

383.   Brophy, "An Early Manchu Account of the Western Regions," 2016–2017.
384.   Newby, "The Empire and the Khanate: A Study of Qing Colonial Administration in Central Asia," 2005.
385.   Ibid.
386.   Ibid.
387.   Kim, Hodong, *The Mongol Empire and Its Legacy*, Brill, 1999.
388.   Millward, James A., *Eurasian Crossroads: A History of Xinjiang*, Columbia University Press, 2007.
389.   Brophy, David, *Uyghur Nation: Reform and Revolution on the Russia-China Frontier*, Harvard University Press, 2016.
390.   Ibid.
391.   Noda, J., "The Ili Sultanate and Its Historical Role," Chikyu Academic Research Papers, 2008.
392.   Kim, H. J., *The Early Muslim Revolts in Central Asia*, Brill, 2004.
393.   Ibid.
394.   Perdue, P. C., *China Marches West: The Qing Conquest of Central Eurasia*, Harvard University Press, 2005.
395.   Ibid.
396.   Millward, J., *Eurasian Crossroads: A History of Xinjiang*, Columbia University Press, 2007.
397.   Noda, J., "The Ili Sultanate and Its Historical Role," Chikyu Academic Research Papers, 2008.
398.   Wei Yuan, *Military History of the Western Regions*, 1844.
399.   Brophy, "An Early Manchu Account of the Western Regions," 2016–2017.
400.   Millward, James, *Eurasian Crossroads: A History of Xinjiang*, Columbia University Press, 2007.
401.   Ibid.

From Empires to Exile: A Brief Uyghur History

The First East Turkistan Republic (1933–1934)

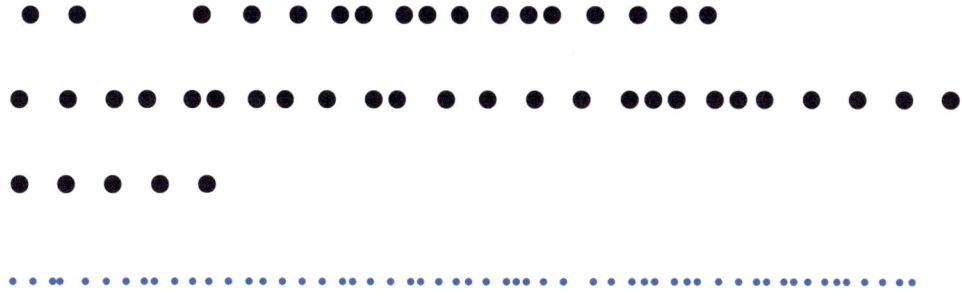

The fall of the Qing Empire in 1912, following the Xinhai Revolution, ended over two centuries of imperial rule.^402 During their dominance, the Manchu rulers governed the Chinese heartland while maintaining a colonial grip over East Turkistan, which they renamed Xinjiang in 1884. Xinjiang means "New Frontier" or "New Territory" in Chinese. After the Qing collapse, East Turkistan became a region of intense contestation due to its strategic location, ethnic diversity, and the vacuum of centralized authority. The competing ambitions of Chinese warlords, Soviet influence, and the growing aspirations of Uyghur and Turkic Muslim populations for self-determination further destabilized governance in the region.

In 1930, the abolition of the Kumul Khanate by Chinese warlord Jin Shuren, coupled with land seizures and forced relocation of Uyghurs to impoverished areas, sparked widespread resentment. These policies deepened economic disparities, leaving many Uyghurs impoverished and dispossessed while further concentrating wealth and land in the hands of Chinese settlers and officials. The socioeconomic impact fueled resistance movements across the region, as Uyghur farmers lost access to arable land, and traditional livelihoods were disrupted. This unrest culminated in the 1931 Kumul Rebellion, led by Khoja Niyaz.^403 The rebellion quickly spread across East Turkistan, with major cities like Khotan also declaring independence, marking a significant moment of unity among resistance movements against Chinese rule.

In 1932, Sabit Damolla Abdulbaqi, a charismatic and deeply religious scholar from Artush near Kashgar, with support from the influential Bughra family in Khotan, organized the Committee for National Revolution. This effort liberated Khotan and established a provisional government. By 1933, the movement had gained strength, bringing together Uyghur and Kyrgyz leaders.^404 On November 12, 1933, the independent Islamic Republic of East Turkistan was proclaimed. Many contemporary Uyghurs and scholars refer to it as the First East Turkistan Republic (ETR).Key leaders included Khoja Niyaz as President, Sabit Damolla Abdulbaqi as Prime Minister, and Mahmut Muhiti as Defense Minister. A 30-article Constitution was adopted, boldly asserting Uyghur identity and sovereignty. The republic, supported by an army of approximately 7,000 troops, was declared in Kashgar, Khotan, and Yarkent in southern East Turkistan. Representing the aspirations of Turkic Muslim populations—Uyghurs, Kazakhs, and Kyrgyz—the First ETR sought independence from Kuomintang-led China and aimed to reclaim the region's identity, religion, and culture.^405

Although the republic lasted a relatively short time, its leaders embodied the vision of an independent East Turkistan. Sabit Damolla Abdulbaqi is remembered for his firm belief in independence, as reflected in his statement:

"We are not Chinese; we are Turkic Muslims, and we must rise to reclaim our land and identity."

Resistance efforts also found support from figures like Mehmet Emin Bughra, a key leader from Khotan, who played a prominent role in both the First and Second East Turkistan Republics (1944–1949). Alongside his brothers Emir Abdullah Bughra and Nur Ahmad Jan Bughra, he led significant resistance efforts in Khotan, driven by the nationalist vision of an independent state. Mehmet Emin Bughra's resolve is captured in his famous saying:

"We will not rest until East Turkistan is free, for without freedom, our faith and future cannot survive."

Despite early successes in resisting Chinese warlords and asserting control over southern East Turkistan, the First ETR faced numerous challenges, including internal divisions, limited resources, and external threats from both the Chinese Nationalist government (Kuomintang) and the Soviet Union. The Soviets, wary of a pan-Islamic or pan-Turkic state near their borders, eventually sided with the Chinese to suppress the republic.

Diplomatic efforts included correspondence with Turkey, Afghanistan, and other nations. However, Turkey's refusal to recognize the republic reflected its alignment with Soviet interests. In January 1934, Soviet-backed Chinese forces, including Hui Muslim warlord Ma Zhongying's troops, launched an assault on Kashgar. The ETR government was forced to withdraw to Yengisar. President Khoja Niyaz fled to the Soviet Union, where he signed an agreement to disband the ETR government, but his cabinet in Yengisar rejected this move. By April 16, 1934, Chinese and Soviet forces overran the republic.

Thousands of civilians were killed during the campaign, including a massacre in Kashgar. Eyewitness accounts describe mass executions, widespread destruction, and the indiscriminate killing of non-combatants, leaving a lasting scar on the city's history. Khoja Niyaz, initially a key leader in the independence movement, negotiated an agreement with the Soviets and Chinese warlord Sheng Shicai, accepting a Chairman position in Sheng's government. His decision, driven by a strategic attempt to preserve East Turkistan's leadership, caused significant controversy. Many viewed it as a betrayal of the independence cause, undermining the unity and resolve of the resistance movement. Prime Minister Sabit Damolla Abdulbaqi rejected the agreement and continued to resist. Sabit Damolla Abdulbaqi and several ministers were later executed under Sheng's orders. These events marked the tragic fall of the First ETR.

The collapse of the First ETR did not end the struggle for independence. In 1937, Defense Minister Mehmut Muhiti organized a rebellion and briefly liberated Kashgar. However, Soviet troops intervened again, deploying air support and ground forces to suppress the uprising. Muhiti fled to Japan, where he sought international backing for East Turkistan's independence but faced limited success.

In November 1937, Khoja Niyaz, who had previously been offered the symbolic position of Honorary Chairman of the Xinjiang Government in Urumchi in 1934 as part of Soviet-mediated negotiations, was arrested and executed in 1938. He had arrived in Urumchi with 120 of his followers, who were also arrested and later executed. Labeled as a counter-revolutionary, "Trotskyist," and "Japanese agent," Khoja Niyaz rejected these charges as fabrications by Sheng Shicai. Facing his sentence, he remarked:

"This death sentence is not new for me. Actually, I have died on the day when I came to Urumchi."[406]

Under Sheng Shicai's rule (1934–1943), East Turkistan became a police state. Thousands of Uyghurs were detained or executed, while mass arrests and repression stifled dissent. Sheng's regime, supported by Soviet advisors, implemented brutal measures, reflecting the ongoing repression Uyghurs face in the region today.

Despite its short existence, the First ETR left a profound legacy. Its emphasis on Uyghur cultural preservation, aspirations for self-determination, and commitment to religious and national identity continue to shape Uyghur movements and inspire contemporary calls for autonomy and recognition. Its leaders, including Sabit Damolla Abdulbaqi, Khoja Niyaz, and Mehmet Emin Bughra, embodied the vision of an independent East Turkistan.

The nationalist and religious ideals that underpinned the First ETR continued to inspire resistance movements for decades. While the republic fell to the combined forces of

Chinese warlords and Soviet intervention, its legacy lives on as a symbol of the strength and unwavering resolve of East Turkistan's people.

The declaration of Independence of First East Turkistan Republic on November 12, 1933 in Kashgar.

Sabit Damolla (3rd right) and other leaders of ETR

ETR Army Officers

The First East Turkistan Republic (1933–1934)

Khoja Niyaz Hajim, The President, with flag of the republic in the back.	Mehmet Emin Bughra, Amir of Khotan.	Sabit Domallo Abdulbaqi, Prime Minister

Notes

402.   Millward, James. Eurasian Crossroads: A History of Xinjiang. New York: Columbia University Press, 2007.
403.   Benson, Linda. The Ili Rebellion: The Moslem Challenge to Chinese Authority in Xinjiang, 1944–1949. Armonk, NY: M. E. Sharpe, 1990.
404.   Forbes, Andrew D. W. Warlords and Muslims in Chinese Central Asia: A Political History of Republican Sinkiang, 1911–1949. Cambridge: Cambridge University Press, 1986.
405.   Bovingdon, Gardner. The Uyghurs: Strangers in Their Own Land. New York: Columbia University Press, 2010.
406.   Pahta, Ghulamuddin. "Soviet-Chinese collaboration in Eastern Turkestan: the case of the 1933 uprising". Institute of Muslim Minority Affairs: 250

154

The Second East Turkistan Republic (ETR) was established in the Ili Valley of East Turkistan in November 1944, exactly 12 years after the establishment of the First ETR.^407 Its creation marked a significant moment for the Turkic Muslim populations in the region, especially the Uyghurs, who sought autonomy from Chinese rule. The short-lived republic's story is complex, involving Soviet intervention, internal divisions, and eventual absorption into communist China..

The roots of the Second ETR lay in long-standing dissatisfaction among the Turkic-speaking peoples of East Turkistan—primarily Uyghurs, Kazakhs, and Kyrgyz—who had been subject to Chinese rule for decades.^407 The Kuomintang (KMT), under warlord Sheng Shicai, controlled East Turkistan with a mixture of harsh repression and Soviet support. However, when Sheng turned against the Soviets in 1942 and aligned himself with the KMT central government, he lost his Soviet backing, leading to widespread discontent across East Turkistan.

This dissatisfaction boiled over into open rebellion in 1944 in the Ili Valley, a region close to the Soviet border. The rebellion quickly spread, and with significant Soviet support, the Turkic Muslim leaders declared the establishment of the Second East Turkistan Republic on November 12, 1944. The ETR controlled the three districts of Ili, Tarbagatai, and Altay, located in the northwestern part of East Turkistan, which bordered the Soviet Union. These regions became the heartland of the ETR, and its influence soon spread across much of East Turkistan.^408

29.1.1 Ilihan Töre's Speech: Call for Independence (1944)

From Empires to Exile: A Brief Uyghur History

On November 12, 1944, Ilihan Töre declared independence of the East Turkistan Republic in Gulja. This is an excerpt (reconstructed based on historical accounts) of his speech:

"We, the people of East Turkistan, have suffered too long under the oppression of Chinese rulers. The time has come for us to unite, to throw off the chains of servitude, and to establish our own republic, where our traditions, our language, and our religion will be preserved. We must stand firm, side by side, as brothers—Uyghurs, Kazakhs, Kyrgyz, and all the Turkic peoples. Together, we will create a new East Turkistan that is free and independent." ^408

• • •• •• • • • • • •• •• •••• • •• • • •••••• • • •• • • • • •• • • • • •••• • •• • • •• •

The leadership of the ETR consisted of individuals with diverse perspectives, ranging from staunch advocates of full independence to those favoring more pragmatic approaches to governance.

- Ilihan Töre: An ardent proponent of complete independence from China, Töre initially served as the chairman of the ETR. His firm stance on sovereignty appealed to those within the republic who prioritized self-determination above all else. However, his unwavering position and vocal criticism of Soviet influence created friction with the Soviets, who sought to align the ETR's goals with their own geopolitical strategy. As a result, Töre's leadership gave way to a more cooperative and moderate figure, Qasimi, whom the Soviets viewed as better suited to their interests.

- Ehmetjan Qasimi: A more moderate figure, Qasimi became the face of the ETR's diplomacy and its primary leader after Töre's fall from favor. Qasimi was an intellectual and an advocate for cooperation with the Soviet Union, realizing that Soviet support was critical for the ETR's survival. Under his leadership, the ETR pursued a strategy of autonomy within a Soviet-backed framework rather than outright independence.

• • •• • • • •• ••• • •• • • •• • • • •• •• •••••• •• •• • • •

The Soviet Union, under Joseph Stalin, played a crucial role in the establishment and early success of the ETR. For Stalin, the creation of a Turkic republic in East Turkistan served multiple purposes. It weakened the KMT's control of the region, secured Soviet influence over a key area in Central Asia, and allowed Moscow to maintain access to the rich natural resources of East Turkistan, including oil, minerals, and agricultural products.^408

The ETR's military achievements were significant. With Soviet assistance, the ETR established a modern army comprising approximately 30,000 to 50,000 troops. These forces were organized into structured divisions, equipped with advanced weaponry such as rifles, artillery, and even some armored vehicles.^408 The ETR's army, trained and advised by Soviet experts, played a crucial role in securing the Ili, Tarbagatai, and Altay regions.^408

The Uyghur population in the region expressed a strong sense of pride and hope about their newfound freedom. For many, the ETR symbolized the possibility of self-governance and the preservation of their cultural identity. The republic's efforts to promote Uyghur language, traditions, and education further reinforced this optimism among its people.^409

Despite these accomplishments, the ETR's ambitions to expand into southern East Turkistan were frustrated. These regions, while ideologically aligned with the ETR, remained under the control of the KMT due to geopolitical and logistical constraints.^408

• • •• •• ••• • • • ••• •• • • • • ••• • • • • ••• • • • • ••• • • • ••• • • •• • • • •

Although the ETR controlled the northwest of East Turkistan, it was unable to extend its military reach into southern regions such as Aksu, Kashgar, and Urumchi—areas that were crucial to the Uyghur population. These regions, while ideologically aligned with the ETR's goals, remained under the control of the KMT, which maintained a stronger military presence there. The inability to advance into these key Uyghur regions can be attributed to several factors:

Geography: The ETR's stronghold in the Ili Valley was far from the more populous and economically important Uyghur regions in the south, such as Kashgar and Aksu. The mountainous terrain and lack of infrastructure made it difficult for the ETR to project military power beyond its immediate borders.^408

Soviet Restraint: While the Soviets provided significant support to the ETR, they were not interested in provoking a full-scale war with the KMT or later the Chinese Communist Party (CCP). Stalin's support was conditional on the ETR not pushing for outright independence or engaging in aggressive territorial expansion that might destabilize Soviet-Chinese relations.^407

Limited Military Resources: Despite Soviet aid, the ETR's military forces were relatively small and poorly equipped compared to the KMT's forces in the south. The ETR could defend its core regions but lacked the manpower and equipment needed to wage a broader campaign in southern East Turkistan.^408

Despite its inability to control the entire Uyghur region, the Second ETR established a functioning government in its territories. The republic created its own military forces, educational systems, and healthcare institutions. The leadership promoted Uyghur and other Turkic cultures, including the use of the Uyghur language in schools and the preservation of Islamic traditions.^410

The ETR's army was one of its notable achievements, transforming into a modern force with Soviet training and equipment. It played a crucial role in securing the Ili region and protecting the republic from external threats.^408 In addition to military advancements, the ETR sought to modernize its economy with Soviet assistance. The Soviets helped develop industries in the Ili region, including agriculture, oil extraction, and mining. Infrastructure projects, such as roads and communication networks, were initiated to bolster connectivity within the republic.^408

Furthermore, the administration prioritized education, establishing new schools that emphasized Uyghur language instruction alongside technical and scientific subjects. This focus on education cultivated a generation of professionals and leaders who contributed to the republic's development.^410 These accomplishments fostered a sense of national identity among Uyghurs and other Turkic groups, resonating with the broader population and symbolizing the potential for self-governance.

The East Turkistan Republic (ETR) forces stopped at the Manas River in 1945, despite being on the brink of capturing Urumchi, due to a shift in Soviet policy and external intervention. Although the ETR forces had successfully routed Chinese Nationalist troops, advanced to the eastern bank of the Manas River, and could have reached Urumchi within days, the Soviets issued orders for the ETR forces to retreat. This decision was strategic and politically motivated.^407

At the time, Urumchi was defenseless, with minimal reinforcements expected to arrive within 8–10 days, and local Chinese leadership was in disarray. The rebellion in Kashgar and surrounding areas further strained Chinese forces. However, the Soviet Union, balancing its international commitments and interests, sought to prevent further escalation. Stalin had initially supported the ETR's independence aspirations but later reassessed the feasibility of an independent East Turkistan given China's strategic importance.^407 The Yalta Agreement and the Sino-Soviet Treaty of Friendship signed in August 1945 compelled the Soviets to prioritize relations with the Chinese Nationalist government over the ETR's ambitions. As Wang Ke notes, this marked a turning point in the fate of the ETR, highlighting the precarious balance of regional geopolitics.^407

• • •• • • • •• • • •• •• • •• • •• •••• • • • •• • • • •• ••• • • • •••• •• • •

In 1946, as the Second World War ended and global political alignments shifted, Stalin re-evaluated his support for the ETR. With the Chinese Civil War intensifying, Stalin sought to maintain stable relations with both the KMT and the CCP. Pressured by the Soviets, the ETR entered into negotiations with the Chinese Nationalist government. The result was the creation of a coalition government in East Turkistan, in which both ETR leaders and Chinese officials held positions of power. This agreement marked the beginning of the ETR's decline. While it allowed the republic to maintain some level of autonomy, it also limited its ability to act independently. The Soviets, eager to avoid a conflict with the rising Chinese Communist Party, began to distance themselves from the ETR's more radical aspirations for full independence.

• • •• • • • •• • • • •• •••• • • • •

By mid-1947 (June), the Chinese Civil War was turning in favor of the CCP, and the ETR's position became increasingly precarious^409. On August 27, 1949, as the CCP prepared to take control of East Turkistan, several key ETR leaders, including Ehmetjan Qasimi, died in a mysterious plane crash while en route to Beijing to negotiate with the communists. The details of the crash remain unclear, but many suspect it was orchestrated by the Soviets to eliminate any potential leaders who might oppose a communist takeover of East Turkistan. Following the death of its leaders on August 27, 1949, the ETR was left leaderless and vulnerable. The Chinese Communist Party, under Mao Zedong, sent the People's Liberation Army (PLA) into East Turkistan in October 1949, arriving in Urumchi on October 20, 1949. By December 20, 1949, the region was firmly under communist control, and the ETR government was officially dissolved on December 22, 1949.

4

From Empires to Exile: A Brief Uyghur History

| Ishakbeg Munonov, the Minister of Defence, and Zunun Tiyip, the Deputy Minister of Defence | ETR Officers | Female Officers |
| Alihan Töre the President. | Ehmentjan Qasimi, the President. | Flag of ETR, the Kokbayraq |

29.9.1 Stalin's Role in Supporting Chinese Control over East Turkistan

The Second East Turkistan Republic (1944-1949): Rise, Peak, Leaders, Soviet Role, and Downfall

On June 27, 1949, Joseph Stalin met with a Chinese Communist Party (CCP) delegation to discuss the future of Xinjiang. During this meeting, Stalin emphasized Xinjiang's strategic importance due to its oil and cotton reserves, vital for China's development.^413 He urged the CCP to act swiftly, warning that delays could invite British interference by rallying Muslim populations, including Indian Muslims, to prolong the civil war.^413 Stalin also recommended increasing the Han Chinese population in Xinjiang from 5% to 30% through resettlement to ensure the region's "all-sided development" and enhance border security.^407

Stalin's advice extended to other border regions, suggesting demographic shifts as a strategy for national defense. Regarding the opposition led by Ma Bufang's cavalry forces, Stalin dismissed them as insignificant, offering Soviet fighter planes to help the CCP neutralize this threat quickly.^413

29.9.2 Mao Zedong's Telegram to Stalin: The Urgency of the Lanzhou-Xi'an Air Route

On September 27, 1949, Mao Zedong sent a telegram to Stalin requesting Soviet assistance in establishing an air route from Urumchi-Lanzhou to Xi'an.^414 Mao outlined the logistical challenges of deploying 500,000 troops into Xinjiang by November, citing poor rail infrastructure, harsh terrain, and limited supplies. He requested 30-50 Soviet transport aircraft, along with crews, fuel, and equipment, to ensure timely troop movement.^414 Mao warned that delays would push deployment to spring, jeopardizing the CCP's plans to consolidate control over Xinjiang.^414.

29.9.3 How East Turkistan's Fate Was Decided

The 1949 communications between Stalin and Mao reveal how global powers determined the future of East Turkistan, prioritizing strategic alliances over local autonomy. Stalin's push for Han resettlement and military intervention facilitated East Turkistan's integration into China, while Mao's reliance on Soviet aid underscored the CCP's dependency on external support.^407 These decisions laid the foundation for systemic demographic and political shifts in the region. The integration of East Turkistan came at a significant cost to the Uyghur people, whose aspirations for autonomy were sacrificed to advance Soviet-Chinese geopolitical objectives.^408.

• • •• • • • • • • • • •• •• • •• ••• • • •••• • •• • • • • • • • •• ••••• ••• • • ••• • •

With the communist takeover, Saypudin Azizi, who had served as a secretary to Ehmetjan Qasimi and worked closely with both the Soviets and the CCP, played a key role in integrating East Turkistan into the People's Republic of China.^407 Azizi became a senior

6

official in the new Xinjiang Uyghur Autonomous Region, which was established in 1955. While the region was granted nominal autonomy, the reality was that it became tightly controlled by Beijing.^409 Azizi's role was controversial; while he promoted Uyghur culture within the communist framework, many saw him as complicit in the erosion of real autonomy for the Uyghurs.^409.

The Second East Turkistan Republic, while short-lived, remains a symbol of Uyghur aspirations for self-determination. Its initial success and Soviet support gave hope to many Uyghurs, but geopolitical realities, Soviet betrayal, and Chinese communist dominance led to its downfall.^410 The ETR's inability to expand its control beyond the Ili region, coupled with the internal divisions within its leadership, limited its long-term potential. The communist takeover of East Turkistan marked the beginning of a new era of repression and assimilation for the Uyghur people.^407 Today, the legacy of the ETR is remembered by Uyghur nationalists as a brief but important moment of autonomy and resistance in their long history of struggle.^410.

Notes

407. Wang Ke, *The East Turkestan Independence Movement, 1930s to 1940s* (Columbia University Press, 2009).
408. James A. Millward, *Eurasian Crossroads: A History of Xinjiang* (New York: Columbia University Press, 2007); Office of the United Nations High Commissioner for Human Rights (OHCHR), *Assessment of Human Rights Concerns in Xinjiang,* August 2022.
409. Joshua Freeman, "Uyghur Genocide and the Global Response," *Foreign Affairs* 100, no. 2 (2022): 50–66.
410. Joanne N. Smith Finley, "The People's Republic of Repression: Xinjiang and the Genocide of Uyghurs," *Journal of Genocide Research* 24, no. 3 (2022): 1–24.
411. Eric Schluessel, *Land of Strangers: The Civilizing Project in Qing Central Asia* (New York: Columbia University Press, 2020).
412. Rian Thum, "The Sacred Routes of Uyghur History," *The Journal of Asian Studies* 73, no. 1 (2014): 1–20.
413. Wilson Center Digital Archive, *Memorandum of Conversation Between Stalin and CCP Delegation,* 27 June 1949. Available at Wilson Center Digital Archive.
414. Wilson Center Digital Archive, *Cable Message from Mao Zedong to Stalin,* 27 September 1949. Available at Wilson Center Digital Archive.
415. Lorenz M. Luthi, *The Sino-Soviet Split: Cold War in the Communist World.*

Ehmetjan Qasimi was a prominent Uyghur leader and one of the most important figures in the history of the Second East Turkistan Republic (ETR). Known for his intellectual approach and pragmatic leadership, Qasimi played a central role in the political and diplomatic struggles of the Uyghur people during the 1940s[416].

Ehmetjan Qasimi was born in 1914 in Ghulja, located in the Ili Valley of East Turkistan, which was part of a region historically inhabited by Uyghurs and other Turkic peoples. He grew up during a time of political turmoil in East Turkistan, which saw the region alternately controlled by Chinese warlords and heavily influenced by the Soviet Union[417]. Qasimi came from an educated family, and his early education set him apart from many of his peers. He studied in the Soviet Union, where he became well-versed in Marxist-Leninist thought, socialist ideology, and modern political theories. His Soviet education not only exposed him to the political strategies of the Soviet Union but also connected him with key political figures in Moscow. His fluency in Russian, Uyghur, and Chinese, along with his intellectual background, made him an effective communicator and mediator[418].

When the Second East Turkistan Republic was established in 1944 in the Ili Valley, Qasimi emerged as a leading figure. He played a crucial role in shaping the political course of the ETR, particularly its relationship with the Soviet Union and the broader regional politics of Central Asia. While Ilihan Töre initially held the position of chairman, advocating for full independence from China, Qasimi's more moderate stance gradually positioned him as the de facto leader of the republic[419].

Ehmetjan Qasimi believed that the survival of the ETR depended on strategic alliances, particularly with the Soviet Union. While he shared the goal of achieving autonomy for Uyghurs and other Turkic peoples, he understood that outright independence would be difficult to achieve given the geopolitical realities of the time. Qasimi's leadership was characterized by his pragmatic approach, recognizing that the republic's future lay in balancing its aspirations for self-rule with the interests of external powers, primarily the Soviet Union and China[420].

Qasimi worked closely with the Soviets, who were sympathetic to the ETR's goals because they wanted to weaken Chinese control over East Turkistan and extend their influence in the region. Under his leadership, the ETR implemented reforms aimed at modernizing education, promoting Uyghur culture and language, and building a socialist-oriented economy with Soviet aid^421.

• • •• • • • • • • • •• •• •••• • •• • • • • ••• •

By 1946, Qasimi had firmly established his leadership of the East Turkistan Republic (ETR), largely supported by the Soviets, who regarded him as a more pragmatic and cooperative leader in contrast to the uncompromising stance of Ilihan Töre. Under his administration, the ETR worked to promote Uyghur culture and language, including the establishment of schools that taught in Uyghur. It also sought to preserve Islamic traditions, which resonated deeply with the predominantly Muslim population, while simultaneously developing a socialist economy with Soviet assistance, particularly in agriculture and industry. Strengthening the republic's military capabilities was another priority, aimed at defending its territory from Kuomintang (KMT) forces and later the Chinese Communist Party (CCP). Under Qasimi's leadership, the ETR solidified its control over the Ili, Altay, and Tarbagatai regions. However, the republic never succeeded in fully expanding into southern East Turkistan, leaving key Uyghur cities in the Tarim basin beyond its reach.^422.

• • •• • • • • ••• ••• • •• ••• ••• • •• • •• • • • •• • • • • • • • ••

In the later years of the ETR, as the Chinese Civil War raged between the Kuomintang (KMT) and the Chinese Communist Party (CCP), the political situation in East Turkistan became more precarious. The Soviet Union, seeking to maintain good relations with both Chinese factions, began pressuring the ETR to negotiate with the KMT government. In 1946, Qasimi participated in the formation of a coalition government in East Turkistan that included representatives from both the ETR and the Chinese government^423. While this coalition granted the ETR a degree of autonomy, it also marked the beginning of the republic's decline. Qasimi was pragmatic in his belief that cooperation with external powers could ensure the long-term survival of the Uyghur people's autonomy. However, as the CCP gained control of China, this strategy became increasingly untenable^424.

• • •• • ••• • ••• • • •• • • •• • • • •• ••• • •• • ••• •

As the Chinese Civil War drew to a close in 1949, the CCP emerged victorious, and East Turkistan's fate was sealed. In August 1949, Ehmetjan Qasimi, along with other key leaders of the ETR, was invited to Beijing to meet with Mao Zedong and negotiate the future of East Turkistan under communist rule. However, on August 27, 1949, the plane

9

carrying Qasimi and several other ETR leaders crashed under mysterious circumstances in the Soviet Union near Lake Baikal^425. The cause of the crash remains unclear, and many historians speculate that it was no accident. Some believe that the Soviets orchestrated the crash to eliminate any potential resistance to the communist takeover of East Turkistan. By removing Qasimi and the other ETR leaders, the Soviets may have sought to smooth the transition of East Turkistan into the People's Republic of China (PRC), which was rapidly consolidating control over the region. With Qasimi's death, the ETR lost its most capable and pragmatic leader. Shortly afterward, the People's Liberation Army (PLA) entered East Turkistan, and by the end of 1949, the region was fully under Chinese communist control^426.

• • •• •• • • • • •• • •   • ••• • •

Ehmetjan Qasimi remains a significant figure in Uyghur history, symbolizing both the aspirations for independency and the complex geopolitical forces that shaped the fate of East Turkistan. His leadership was marked by a careful balance between pursuing autonomy for the Uyghur people and maintaining alliances with external powers. His death, under suspicious circumstances, effectively ended the dream of the Second East Turkistan Republic^427. Qasimi's pragmatic approach, while criticized by some for being too conciliatory, likely prolonged the existence of the ETR and avoided immediate conflict with more powerful actors like the Soviet Union and China.

His diplomatic efforts and vision for a more modern, independent Uyghur state continue to resonate with Uyghur nationalists who view him as a martyr for their cause. Though the republic he led was short-lived, Ehmetjan Qasimi's contributions to the struggle for Uyghur self-determination remain an enduring part of the region's history, representing both the hope for freedom and the geopolitical challenges that prevented its realization.

Notes

416.   Sean Roberts, *The War on the Uyghurs: China's Internal Campaign Against a Muslim Minority* (Princeton: Princeton University Press, 2020).
417.   James A. Millward, *Eurasian Crossroads: A History of Xinjiang* (New York: Columbia University Press, 2007).
418.   Eric Schluessel, *Land of Strangers: The Civilizing Project in Qing Central Asia* (New York: Columbia University Press, 2020).
419.   Joanne N. Smith Finley, "The People's Republic of Repression: Xinjiang and the Genocide of Uyghurs," *Journal of Genocide Research* 24, no. 3 (2022): 1–24.
420.   Joshua Freeman, "Uyghur Genocide and the Global Response," *Foreign Affairs* 100, no. 2 (2022): 50–66.
421.   Rian Thum, "The Sacred Routes of Uyghur History," *The Journal of Asian Studies* 73, no. 1 (2014): 1–20.
422.   Wilson Center Digital Archive, "Memorandum of Conversation Between Stalin and CCP Delegation," 27 June 1949. Available at Wilson Center Digital Archive.

423. Wilson Center Digital Archive, "Cable Message from Mao Zedong to Stalin, 27 September 1949." Available at Wilson Center Digital Archive.
424. Lorenz M. Luthi, *The Sino-Soviet Split: Cold War in the Communist World* (Princeton: Princeton University Press, 2008).
425. Peter C. Perdue, *China Marches West: The Qing Conquest of Central Eurasia* (Harvard: Harvard University Press, 2005).
426. Office of the United Nations High Commissioner for Human Rights (OHCHR), "Assessment of Human Rights Concerns in Xinjiang," August 2022.
427. James A. Millward, *Eurasian Crossroads: A History of Xinjiang* (New York: Columbia University Press, 2007).

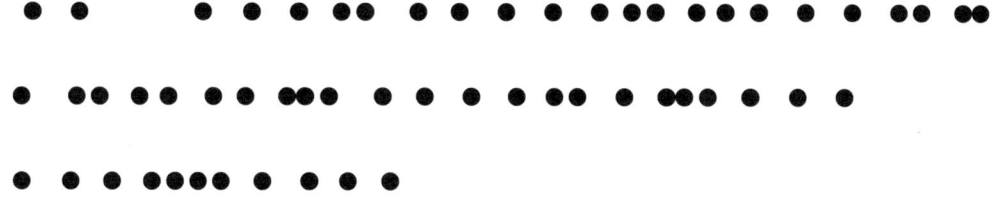

The history of the Uyghurs following the communist takeover in 1949 marks the beginning of a long and tragic struggle for survival as a people. After the newly established Chinese Communist Party, under Mao Zedong, absorbed the region of East Turkistan—it renamed it the Xinjiang Uyghur Autonomous Region (XUAR). Mao's campaigns, particularly during the Cultural Revolution (1966–1976), intensified repression, demolishing mosques, persecuting religious leaders, and criminalizing traditional practices^428. These early years of control eroded Uyghur cultural and religious life, setting the stage for an even more severe campaign of suppression in the 21st century.

The most difficult period in Uyghur history has been the ongoing genocide and mass atrocities that began in 2016 under the current Chinese government. Using counterterrorism as a justification, the Chinese government launched a sweeping crackdown on the Uyghur population in East Turkistan. Between 1 million and 1.5 million Uyghurs—approximately 8–12% of the Uyghur population—have been detained in a vast network of detention camps, officially referred to as "vocational education and training centers." Here, Uyghurs are subjected to forced indoctrination, torture, forced labor, and sterilization^429. Outside the camps, Uyghurs live under the constant scrutiny of a surveillance state that monitors their movements and communications and restricts their religious and cultural practices^430.

The Chinese government asserts that these measures are necessary to combat extremism and terrorism in East Turkistan. Officials claim that the policies are designed to provide education and job training, thus improving socioeconomic conditions and fostering stability. However, international experts, including Sean Roberts in *The War on the Uyghurs*, argue that China's use of counterterrorism rhetoric is a thinly veiled strategy to eliminate Uyghur culture^431. Roberts traces how China exploited global fears of terrorism after 9/11 to justify its brutal policies against the Uyghurs, despite limited evidence of Uyghur extremism. This framing has allowed China to brand Uyghurs as "terrorists" and "extremists" on the international stage, concealing a broader agenda of forced assimilation and cultural annihilation.

In response, the United Nations and global human rights organizations have expressed deep concern. In August 2022, the Office of the UN High Commissioner for Human

Rights (OHCHR) published a landmark report that highlighted credible evidence of crimes against humanity in East Turkistan, including arbitrary detention, torture, forced labor, and forced sterilization^432. The report urged China to release all detainees, underscoring that the mass detentions have no legal basis and are aimed at dismantling Uyghur culture and religion. Despite this, diplomatic divisions within the UN have complicated efforts to hold China accountable, as economic interests have led some nations to remain silent on the atrocities^433.

Many scholars and international human rights organizations have condemned the persecution of the Uyghurs as both a human rights crisis and a moral issue for the global Muslim community. Yet, due to complex geopolitical and economic factors, many Muslim-majority governments have refrained from taking a strong stance, highlighting the challenges of confronting China's policies^434.

Despite facing one of the darkest periods in their history, the Uyghur people continue to demonstrate remarkable resilience. Historian James Millward, in his book *Eurasian Crossroads: A History of Xinjiang*, explores the Uyghurs' deep cultural roots in Central Asia and emphasizes the enduring resilience of their identity^435. Millward's analysis sheds light on how, despite efforts to erode their culture, the Uyghurs' commitment to preserving their language, traditions, and faith has remained steadfast. From exiled Uyghur communities preserving their heritage to individuals documenting and exposing the crisis, the Uyghurs have shown that their identity remains strong and unbreakable. The international awareness generated by the UN report and the work of activists offers hope that justice can still be achieved^436.

In the face of immense suffering, the Uyghur spirit has not been broken. Their determination to maintain their history, language, and culture amidst a campaign of genocide stands as a testament to human fortitude and the power of unity. As international support grows and advocacy intensifies, there is hope that the Uyghurs will emerge from this tragedy with their culture intact and their future reclaimed. Through unity, perseverance, and the unwavering commitment to their identity, the Uyghur people embody a legacy of strength and determination that will endure.

Notes

428.   Sean Roberts, *The War on the Uyghurs: China's Internal Campaign Against a Muslim Minority* (Princeton: Princeton University Press, 2020).
429.   Office of the United Nations High Commissioner for Human Rights (OHCHR), "Assessment of Human Rights Concerns in Xinjiang," August 2022. Available at ohchr.org.
430.   Council on Foreign Relations, "China's Repression of Uyghurs in Xinjiang," 2023. Available at cfr.org.
431.   Sean Roberts, *The War on the Uyghurs: China's Internal Campaign Against a Muslim Minority* (Princeton: Princeton University Press, 2020).

432. Joshua Freeman, "Uyghur Genocide and the Global Response," *Foreign Affairs* 100, no. 2 (2022): 50–66.

433. Joanne N. Smith Finley, "The People's Republic of Repression: Xinjiang and the Genocide of Uyghurs," *Journal of Genocide Research* 24, no. 3 (2022): 1–24.

434. Eric Schluessel, *Land of Strangers: The Civilizing Project in Qing Central Asia* (New York: Columbia University Press, 2020).

435. James A. Millward, *Eurasian Crossroads: A History of Xinjiang* (New York: Columbia University Press, 2007).

436. Rian Thum, "The Sacred Routes of Uyghur History," *The Journal of Asian Studies* 73, no. 1 (2014): 1–20.

437. Uyghur Human Rights Project, "Concentration Camps in China: Uyghurs and Other Turkic Peoples," 2023. Available at uhrp.org.

• ••• •• • ••

Finally, let this book serve not only as a testament to the resilience and enduring spirit of the Uyghur people but also as a call to action: a plea for a world where diversity is cherished, history is preserved, and every individual can live with dignity, freedom, and peace. In honoring their story, we reaffirm the shared humanity that binds us all—a reminder that understanding and compassion are the bridges to a brighter, more just future.

Made in the USA
Columbia, SC
23 February 2025